Canadian Fishing Cookbook

Jeff Morrison
and James Darcy

www.companyscoming.com
visit our website

First Printing November 2012

Library and Archives Canada Cataloguing in Publication
Morrison, Jeff, 1967–
        Canadian fishing cookbook / Jeff Morrison & James Darcy.
(Wild Canada series)
Includes index.
ISBN 978-1-897477-67-0
        1. Cooking (Fish). 2. Cookbooks. I. Darcy, James II. Title.
III. Series: Wild Canada series
TX747.M844 2013   641.6'92   C2012-906884-5

Published by
Company's Coming Publishing Limited
2311–96 Street NW
Edmonton, Alberta, Canada T6N 1G3
Tel: 780-450-6223   Fax: 780-450-1857
www.companyscoming.com

Cover image: © Jörn Rynio, Rights Managed

We gratefully acknowledge the following supplier for their generous support of our Test and Photography Kitchens: Campers' Village (p. 88).

Company's Coming is a registered trademark owned by Company's Coming Publishing Limited.

We acknowledge the financial support of the Government of Canada through the Canada Book Fund for our publishing activities.

Printed in China

PC: 21

Table of Contents

Introduction

Canada prides itself on a special connection to its renewable natural resources. Living close to the land, as we have always done, gives our country and its people a deep appreciation for fish and wildlife, something steeped in our natural heritage and tradition. An intertwined network of streams and rivers runs through our country, and our topography is generously dotted with kettle ponds and lakes as far as the eye can see. Canada, in fact, boasts one-quarter of the world's wetlands and in this ubiquitous water lurks wild fish species as strange and as beautiful as our land itself.

The plethora of different fish found in this great country is staggering, providing its citizens with a seemingly endless gastronomic delight. Today, when healthy eating is of utmost importance, the consumption of fish in our diet—especially wild strains of Canadian fish from sea to sea—has never been so crucial. Whether you prefer sport fishing as a tool for bringing that healthy, nutritious meal to the table, or would rather purchase fresh from the fish market, I can say with experience that this country has some of the finest-tasting fish of anywhere in the world. I have been fortunate enough to travel this great land, not only as an avid sport fisherman but as a lover of wild fish and game. From freshly jigged cod in Seal Cove, Newfoundland, to smoked coho salmon in Campbell River, British Columbia, to pan-seared pike in northern Québec, to unforgettable walleye fries in central Ontario, I have enjoyed the pleasures of our precious *poisson* from the fishing rod to the table.

Easy access to fresh, wild Canadian fish is really only half the battle we face in this country. Learning the different ways to prepare and serve this incredible renewable bounty can sometimes be a daunting task. In this book, you will discover not only some of the best-kept fish-cooking secrets from east to west and from north to south, but you will also learn a multitude of different ways to prepare fish for you and your family, as I have. The recipes I have selected for this book are as diverse and unique as our country itself. They cover a virtual cornucopia of regional tastes and represent, I believe, what cooking and eating wild fish is all about. For those of you who enjoy eating what you catch, the *Canadian Fishing Cookbook* will surely come in handy. And those who simply enjoy a tasty, well-thought-out fish meal will be in their glory.

Cooking wild fish requires little more than the ability to catch a fish and read a recipe, and I have a few tips that will help you along the way.

Most wild fish will need to be cleaned and filleted; some need boning and some need skinning. Many processes that are specific to certain types of fish (such as skinning a catfish) are described in Tips throughout this book.

Cleaning a Fish

"Cleaning" a fish implies that it is gutted and washed. To properly clean a fish, start with a good, sharp fillet knife. Begin at the tail and insert the knife into the fish's vent. With a smooth forward stroke, cut through to the centre of the belly to the middle of the gill plate, making sure not to cut too deep. Remove the gills completely, eviscerate the entire fish and discard the organs. Rinse the fish under cold water, and then remove the kidneys (which run along the inside of the backbone) with the end of your thumbnail. Rinse again under cold water and make sure the body cavity is clean and free of debris. Do not remove the head unless the recipe calls for it.

Filleting a Fish

There are several ways to fillet a fish. Here is one technique that works well for both small and large fish.

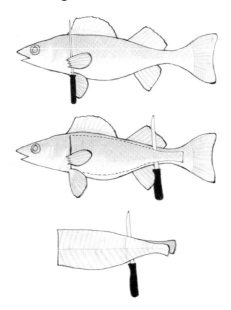

1. Cut a slit behind the fish's pectoral fin. You may cut off the head completely if you prefer.

2. Hold the fish by the tail or clamp the fish down on a wooden fillet board. With your fillet knife blade pointing away from you and across the body of the fish, begin to cut from the tail toward the head.

3. To separate the fillet from the skin, begin by holding the fillet by the tail-end with your thumb and forefinger, or with a pair of pliers. Skin should always be facing down.

4. Insert the knife between the skin and the flesh and slowly cut forward with long, smooth strokes. You will need a slightly downward motion to separate the meat at the skin. Be careful not to cut through the skin.

5. Continue your cut through to the end until skin is separated from the meat. Discard the skin and rinse the fillet under cool water.

Cooking Wild Fish

There are a number of ways that you can cook your wild fish dishes. Some recipes in this book require a conventional oven, and so are most easily prepared at home, but many cottages, cabins and camps have ovens as well. Use a meat thermometer to gauge an unfamiliar oven's temperature. Other recipes in this book are ideal for cooking outside: on the barbecue, camp stove, or right over the open fire! A campfire suitable for cooking is one that has burnt down to a bed of nice, hot coals, which usually takes at least one hour.

Ingredients and Tools

Experienced fishermen and campers know to think ahead and bring what they need with them. If you'll be cooking in the outdoors, make sure to read through the recipes in advance and make a list of the ingredients and kitchen tools you'll need.

Most recipes don't require much beyond basic implements, such as knives, forks, spoons, flippers, ladles, and pots and pans (including a Dutch oven). Double-check your recipe in advance to make sure that nothing extra is needed.

There are a few small items and cooking utensils one should always have when travelling into the backwoods: aluminum foil, non-stick cooking spray, skewers (metal and wood), oven mitts or pot holders, fire igniter, extra cooking oil, paper towels, a paring knife, a fillet knife, a meat saw, scissors, an axe, a shovel and a camping cooler.

Make sure to store your food in a safe place, such as a vehicle or suspended by ropes in a tree. Discard of any wild fish leftovers properly and don't leave any food lying around.

A Few Helpful Tips

Western Baked Clams

Serves 6

Vancouver's Fish House Restaurant at Stanley Park is known for its clams and mussels, and executive chef Karen Barnaby has learned more than a few tricks while cooking at the famous eatery. "Most people discard clams and mussels that don't open during cooking, thinking that they have gone bad," explains Barnaby. "But really, the time to root out bad clams and mussels is before they're even cooked." Chef Barnaby, who has been the Fish House's executive chef since 1995, suggests you first place your clams and mussels in a bowl and jostle them around. If any do not close, simply discard them.

6 large clams in shells

12 unsalted soda crackers, crushed
3 Tbsp (45 mL) garlic powder
2 Tbsp (30 mL) parsley

1/2 cup (125 mL) butter

1 tsp (5 mL) lemon juice (optional)
dash of hot pepper sauce (optional)

In saucepan, boil clams for about 5 minutes until they open. Discard any clams that do not open. Drain and remove half of shell from each clam. Place sides of clam shell with meat on rimmed baking sheet.

Combine crackers, garlic powder and parsley in sealable plastic bag and crush until fine.

Melt butter in frying pan on medium and add cracker crumb mixture. Cook until golden brown, stirring constantly. Spoon mixture onto clams on baking sheet.

Preheat oven to 350°F (175°C). Bake clams for 10 to 15 minutes until topping has browned. Remove from oven and sprinkle with lemon juice and hot pepper sauce if desired. Serve immediately.

PEI Crab Scoops

Makes 16 appetizers

Crab is one of Canada's most valuable seafood exports, contributing nearly $1 billion to the economy each year. Dungeness and red rock crabs are harvested extensively on the West Coast. Dungeness crabs must be at least

6.5 inches (16.5 centimetres) across the widest part of their shell, and red rock crabs should measure a minimum of 4.5 inches (11.4 centimetres). In the crab industry, female crabs are protected and must be released by fishermen. A single female crab may produce over 2 million eggs at one time.

> **2 PEI potatoes, peeled, boiled and mashed**
> **8 oz (225 g) crabmeat**
> **3 chives, finely chopped**
> **1 tsp (5 mL) chopped fresh thyme**
> **1/2 tsp (2 mL) Dijon mustard**
> **1/2 fresh green chili pepper, seeded and finely chopped**
> **1 egg, lightly beaten**
> **1/2 tsp (2 mL) salt**
> **pepper, to taste**
>
> **1/2 cup (125 mL) flour**
> **2 cups (500 mL) canola oil**
>
> **dip or salsa, to serve**

Place mashed potatoes in medium bowl; add crabmeat, chives, thyme, mustard, chili pepper, egg, salt and pepper. Mix well and cover; refrigerate for 1 hour.

Remove from refrigerator and use your hands to roll crabmeat mixture into small "golf balls." Sprinkle each lightly with flour. Heat oil on medium-high in large skillet. Add crab scoops and fry until golden brown.

Transfer crab scoops to paper towel–lined plate to drain, then to serving platter. Serve hot with dip or salsa.

Try with This  **Easy Fish Dip**
Makes 1/2 cup (125 mL)

1/2 cup (125 mL) mayonnaise
1 tsp (5 mL) ground Italian seasoning
1 tsp (5 mL) granulated garlic
1 Tbsp (15 mL) prepared yellow mustard
1 1/2 tsp (7 mL) lemon juice
1 Tbsp (15 mL) minced green onion
dash of salt
dash of pepper
dash of paprika

Mix ingredients together in small bowl. Use as topping or dip for any fish.

Baked and Broiled Mackerel

Serves 4

Fishing enthusiast Grant Bailey of Ottawa spends much of the summer at his cottage in Prince Edward Island, where he enjoys fishing for and eating mackerel. Grant says mackerel are easy to catch and there are lots of them around. From wharves and piers in mid-July, prospectors of these fish, like Grant, will be found casting the harbours hoping to strike gold. By mid-August, though, the "macks" have started heading into the bays, where Grant is able to catch them off the pier in Souris, PEI. The tackle he uses is a three-fly leader with a lure attached to the end. After spawning, these fast-swimming fish are on the feed, moving constantly in search of almost any available food source. The key, according to Grant Bailey, is a rising tide and clear water.

> **1/4 cup (60 mL) salt**
> **1/2 cup (125 mL) sugar**
> **4 mackerel fillets**
> **1/2 cup (125 mL) maple syrup,** *divided*
> **1/2 cup (125 mL) olive oil,** *divided*

Preheat oven to 300°F (150°C). Mix salt and sugar together and coat each mackerel fillet well, making sure to cover the whole fillet. Place mackerel in baking pan and drizzle with 1/4 cup (60 mL) maple syrup and 1/4 cup (60 mL) oil. Bake, uncovered, for 12 to 15 minutes until cooked. Remove pan from oven and set oven to broil.

Coat mackerel with remaining maple syrup and oil. Broil about 4 to 5 inches (10 to 12 cm) from top element for about 2 to 3 minutes until outside of mackerel is crispy and nearly black. Fillets may be served whole as an entrée or sliced into strips as an appetizer.

Try with This  ## Carrots in Dill Butter

Serves 6

8 carrots, peeled and sliced into 1-inch (2.5 cm) pieces
1/2 cup (125 mL) water
2 Tbsp (30 mL) butter
1 tsp (5 mL) white sugar
1/2 tsp (2 mL) salt
1/2 tsp (2 mL) dill seed

Combine all ingredients in medium saucepan. Bring to a boil and then reduce heat. Simmer for 25 to 30 minutes until carrots are tender.

Smoked Salmon Pâté

Serves 8

When smoking salmon, the first question that comes to mind is what wood to use? Since it is such a hot topic among the "smoking community," I can tell you that there is no single correct answer to this question. According to the experts, a variety of different woods can be used, except for treated wood and pine—pine contains resins that will make your fish taste bitter. A few common woods used for smoking fish are alder, hickory, oak, apple and any other fruit or nut wood. How long should your fish remain in the smoker? The rule of thumb is about one hour for thin fillets, and as much as four hours for larger, thicker fish fillets. As with other cooking methods, practice makes perfect and it may take a batch or two before you fine-tune your smoking. As with frying or other methods, the flesh is usually done when it flakes easily with a fork.

> 3 cups (750 mL) smoked salmon or halibut,
>   broken into small pieces
> 1 1/2 cups (375 mL) soft, room-temperature
>   cream cheese, cut into large cubes
> 8 dashes of hot red pepper sauce
>   (add 4 extra dashes if using halibut)
> 2 Tbsp (30 mL) lemon juice
>   (add 1 more Tbsp [15 mL] if using halibut)
> 2 Tbsp (30 mL) dill
> salt and pepper, to taste
> fresh dill and lemon slices, for garnish

Break fish into small pieces and combine with all ingredients, except garnish, in food processor. Process for about 3 minutes until smooth. Pour into mould or bowl lined with plastic wrap. Refrigerate for at least 2 hours. Turn mould over and remove wrap. Smooth with knife and decorate as desired with dill and lemon slices. Serve with your choice of bread or crackers.

Smoked Trout Roll-ups

Makes 24 appetizer servings

According to Agriculture and Agri-Food Canada, trout are farmed extensively in six provinces, with Ontario being the leading producer of commercial rainbow trout. In 2006, Ontario produced 4250 tonnes of rainbow trout valued at more than $16 million and representing approximately 80 percent of the entire Canadian output of farmed rainbow trout. Ontario hatchery facilities tend to focus on intensive recirculation systems, flow-through hatcheries and occasionally cage and pond rearing.

> 4 oz (115 g) smoked trout fillets, skin discarded
>   and fish broken into pieces
> 1/4 cup (60 mL) soft cream cheese
> 2 Tbsp (30 mL) chopped fresh dill
> 2 Tbsp (30 mL) mayonnaise
> 1 Tbsp (15 mL) lemon juice
> 1 Tbsp (15 mL) horseradish
> 1/4 tsp (1 mL) pepper
> 4 large tortillas
> 1 English cucumber, thinly sliced
> 3/4 cup (175 mL) minced red pepper

Place trout, cream cheese, dill, mayonnaise, lemon juice, horseradish and pepper in food processor and purée until smooth. Divide trout mixture among tortillas; place cucumber slices over top and sprinkle with red pepper. Roll up tightly and cut into 3/4-inch (2 cm) pieces. You can wrap and chill roll-ups for up to 24 hours before serving.

Arctic Char Chowder

Serves 4 to 6

Arctic char, like many other coldwater fish, are game fish that are highly prized for their sporting abilities as well as for table fare. In the northern rivers of Québec, fishermen usually catch char by using medium- to heavy-spinning equipment. Since char are piscivorous (they feed extensively on smaller bait fish), anglers often use brightly coloured spoons and spinners to imitate the natural feed in the Arctic char's diet. Anglers often fish from the shore or anchor a short distance out in the river and cast lures in typical char holding areas, such as small backwater bays, eddies or slack water areas behind large boulders. Char are great fighters and provide anglers a real challenge on hook and line.

> 1 1/2 lbs (680 g) thick Arctic char or wild salmon fillets (*see* Tip)
> salt and pepper, to taste
> 1/4 cup (60 mL) butter
> 1/2 cup (125 mL) chopped onion
> 1/2 cup (125 mL) chopped carrots
> 1/2 cup (125 mL) chopped celery
>
> 1 1/2 cups (375 mL) vegetable broth
> 28 oz (796 mL) can crushed tomatoes
> 1/2 tsp (2 mL) thyme
> 1 bay leaf
>
> 1/2 cup (125 mL) whipping cream (optional)

Bone fillets and remove skin from fish. Cut fish into 3/4-inch (2 cm) cubes; sprinkle with salt and pepper. In pot over medium, melt butter and cook onion, carrots and celery for about 5 minutes.

Add broth, tomatoes, thyme and bay leaf, and cover and simmer for 15 minutes.

Add fish; gently stir in cream if desired. Simmer, uncovered, for 15 minutes more, stirring occasionally. Remove bay leaf and adjust seasoning to taste.

 tip   Thicker fillets are easier to cube than thinner fillets.

Nova Scotia Clam Chowder

Serves 4

Did you know that Atlantic clams remain buried in the mud throughout the tide cycle? They actually have a specialized retractable siphon that can be extended to the surface when the tide is in, or retracted when the tide is out. These clams are the ones that squirt water upward when you walk over tide flats. Clams are dug by hand with a fork or clam hack. The clams are collected in a "kibben," a wooden slated box with a handle—today's version is often made of plastic milk crates. Clam flats are regularly monitored for toxic algal blooms and fecal bacteria. Notices are posted when clams should not be dug. These clams have a variety of other names including steamers, and are often served deep-fried, baked or as-is after steaming. A licence must be purchased to commercially harvest clams.

3 × 5 oz (142 g) cans clams, drained, with juice reserved
2 cups (500 mL) cubed potatoes (1-inch [2.5 cm] cubes)
1 cup (250 mL) diced celery
1/2 cup (125 mL) water

3/4 cup (175 mL) butter
3/4 cup (175 mL) flour
1 cup (250 mL) cream (18%)
2 cups (500 mL) milk
2 tsp (10 mL) salt
pepper, to taste

oyster crackers, to serve

In large skillet over medium, add juice from clams, potato cubes, celery and water. Cook until potatoes soften.

In medium saucepan over medium, mix butter, flour, cream and milk. Cook until smooth, stirring to keep from sticking. Add potato and celery mixture and clams; season with salt and pepper. Cover and let simmer for 10 minutes until chowder is smooth and creamy. Serve with oyster crackers.

Potato Fish Chowder

Serves 8

While you're enjoying your fish chowder, did you know that Canada boasts one of the world's most comprehensive fish inspection systems? The Canadian Food Inspection Agency (CFIA) in Ottawa establishes regulatory requirements for all fish products and seafood-processing establishments across the country, as well as commercial fishing vessels and all equipment used in storing and transporting fish products. My sister Cheryl Ann just happens to be one of the analysts with the CFIA in Ottawa.

3 strips bacon

2 Tbsp (30 mL) butter
1 small leek (white and light green parts only), diced
1 onion, diced
1 celery rib, diced
1 bay leaf
1 garlic clove
1/2 red pepper, diced
1/4 tsp (1 mL) salt
1/4 tsp (1 mL) paprika
3 Tbsp (45 mL) flour
2 × 8 1/2 oz (240 mL) bottles clam juice
1 potato, peeled and thinly sliced

1 1/2 cups (375 mL) milk
12 oz (340 g) cod or halibut fillets,
    cut into 1-inch (2.5 cm) pieces

2 Tbsp (30 mL) chopped fresh parsley

Cook bacon strips until crisp. Drain on paper towel, crumble and set aside.

Melt butter in large saucepan over medium. Add leek, onion, celery, bay leaf, garlic, red pepper, salt and paprika, and cook for about 5 minutes, stirring occasionally, until leek and onion have softened. Stir in flour. Cook for 2 minutes, stirring often. Stir in clam juice and bring mixture to a boil. Add potato. Cover saucepan and simmer over medium for about 10 minutes.

Add milk and return to a simmer. Add fish and continue simmering for about 5 minutes until fish flakes easily. Remove and discard bay leaf. Serve in individual soup bowls; sprinkle with parsley and crumbled bacon.

Perch Chowder

Serves 6

Using a slow cooker for fish has many advantages, including an extended cooking time that allows for better distribution of flavour. The lower temperatures lessen the chance of scorching foods that tend to stick to the bottom of a pan and burn easily in an oven. The slow cooker also frees your oven and stovetop for other uses, and should definitely be considered an option for large gatherings or holiday meals. For many recipes, a slow cooker can be left unattended all day. You can also put ingredients into a slow cooker before going to work and come home to a hot meal.

1 medium onion, chopped
1 Tbsp (15 mL) butter
2 cups (500 mL) milk
1 cup (250 mL) ranch dressing
1 lb (454 g) boneless perch fillets
1 × 10 oz (280 g) package frozen broccoli florets, thawed
2 cups (500 mL) cubed or shredded Cheddar cheese
1/4 tsp (1 mL) garlic powder
oyster crackers, to serve

Sauté onion and butter in medium skillet until tender. In slow cooker, add milk, ranch dressing, fish, broccoli, cheese and garlic powder. Place lid on slow cooker and cook on high for 2 hours, stirring occasionally. Chowder is done when fish flakes easily with a fork and a creamy consistency is reached. Serve with oyster crackers.

Try with This  **Canadian Tea Biscuits**

Makes 12

3 cups (750 mL) self-rising flour
1/2 cup (125 mL) all-purpose flour
1/2 tsp (2 mL) sugar
1/4 cup (60 mL) butter
3/4 cup (175 mL) milk
1 egg

Preheat oven to 400°F (205°C). Mix flours and sugar in large bowl. Cut butter into small chunks, add to flour mixture and stir to blend. In separate bowl, whisk together milk and egg and add to batter. Stir until mixture becomes doughy.

Lightly flour work surface and knead dough gently. Flatten dough to about 1/2-inch (12 mm) thick and cut into biscuits with knife or cookie cutter. Place biscuits on greased baking sheets. Bake for about 15 minutes until golden brown.

Beaven Lake Bisque

Serves 4 to 6

My good friends Jim and Sharron Bindon live on the shores of Québec's beautiful Beaven Lake, a most pristine body of water nestled in a picturesque valley of the famous Laurentian Mountains. Beaven Lake has always been my home waters—a lake I have fished since I was a boy, and where I've spent many long hours swimming and enjoying water sports at the Morrison family beach. The Bindons' tasty bisque recipe is one I have enjoyed immensely, and though we usually make it with northern pike caught from our favourite lake, any fish species could be used. For me, however, there is no substitution for Beaven Lake pike in this memorable bisque that brings me back home every time I have it. This meal is best enjoyed with oyster crackers, and if you're like us, a big jar of pickled pork tongues on the side.

> 1 × 10 oz (284 mL) can condensed tomato soup
> 1 × 10 oz (284 mL) can condensed cream of celery soup
> 1 × 10 oz (284 mL) can condensed cream of mushroom soup
> 1 × 10 oz (284 mL) can condensed green pea soup
> 5 cups (1.25 L) milk
> 1 × 7 1/2 oz (213 g) can crabmeat, undrained
> 1 cup (250 mL) Beaven Lake northern pike
>   (or your choice of fish), cubed and slightly pan-seared
> 1 tsp (5 mL) salt
>
> paprika, for sprinkling
> 1/4 cup (60 mL) chopped parsley

Combine all 4 canned soups in large pot and blend. Gradually add milk. Add crabmeat, fish and salt. Heat slowly, stirring constantly (the mixture scorches easily so keep stirring), until just hot enough to serve. Sprinkle with paprika and parsley and serve.

Crab Salad with Tomatoes

Serves 6

In my research, I have discovered a rather easy way to prepare crab for the table. After crab are cooked, start by first removing the back, then hold the base of the crab with one hand and pull the shell away from the body with the other hand. Turn your crab over and pull on the triangular-shaped section and lift it away, then gently scrape away the gills on either side with a spoon. Throw away the intestines, which run down the centre of the back. You may also choose to wash away the yellow material often called "crab butter." Then twist off the legs, rinse the rest of the body under cold water and break it in half. Now your delicious crab is ready for eating!

> 2 lbs (900 g) crabmeat
> 1/4 cup (60 mL) chopped shallots
> 1/4 cup (60 mL) diced red pepper
> 1/2 cup (125 mL) sour cream
> 1 celery rib, diced
> salt and pepper, to taste
>
> 6 tomatoes, thickly sliced
> balsamic vinegar, for drizzling

In bowl, combine crabmeat with shallots, red pepper, sour cream and celery. Mix well. Season with salt and pepper.

Spread half of tomato slices in 1 layer on large serving platter. Add thin layer of crab mixture. Spread tomatoes on top, and add another layer of crab on that. Slowly drizzle with balsamic vinegar. Serve immediately.

Herring Salad

Serves 4

The herring is a small, oily fish that is very high in important omega-3 fatty acids—it is a great source of "brain food." Some people are not fond of herring because it is oily, but it is frequently served smoked or pickled and is enjoyed across the country. When served in a salad or as a sandwich spread, it is often mistaken for tuna. This fish, along with its many cooking techniques, has been an important food in many cultures since 3000 BC. Herring are also readily found in many fish markets, and in Canada we have several members of the herring family roaming our waters: the alewife, the American shad and the gizzard shad.

> 4 large herrings, backbones removed (*see* Tip, p. 103)
> 4 large potatoes, cooked and diced
> 1 beet, cooked and diced
> 1 small onion, grated
> 2 Fuji or Gala apples, chopped
> 4 gherkins, chopped
> 2 Tbsp (30 mL) vinegar
> 1/2 tsp (2 mL) salt
> 1/2 tsp (2 mL) pepper
>
> 1 or 2 hard-boiled eggs, peeled
> parsley, for garnish

Preheat oven to 400°F (205°C). Cover herrings with greaseproof paper and bake for 10 minutes. Once fish have cooled, cut into small pieces, taking off skin and removing any bones. Mix with potatoes, beet, onion, apples, gherkins, vinegar, salt and pepper.

Form mixture into attractive shape, or pack tightly into a mould. Refrigerate for 1 hour. Meanwhile, cut hard-boiled eggs into halves; cover and refrigerate.

Turn mould out onto platter; garnish with hard-boiled egg shapes and parsley.

Salmon Salad

Serves 4

The fishing in Lake Ontario has grown greatly in popularity over the years, and that is mostly because of the salmon. Anglers come from far and wide to fish the lake in hopes of hooking a good-sized chinook or coho. I can recall a charter fishing trip I did out of Bath, Ontario, near Kingston. My friends and I caught many lake trout but only a few salmon. It wasn't difficult to tell when you had a salmon on the line, and the charter boat operator knew right away. If your rod bent over slightly and bounced the instant the down-rigger went off, it was a lake trout; but if the rod doubled over and the drag started "screaming," you knew you had a salmon. Salmon are considered one of the hardest-fighting fish in the world, and on that trip to Lake Ontario, I learned that firsthand.

> 2 cups (500 mL) cooked salmon, flaked (or canned; drain well)
> 2 hard-boiled eggs, peeled and diced
> 1/2 English cucumber, peeled and diced
> 1 red pepper, diced
> 1 green pepper, diced
> 1/3 cup (75 mL) mayonnaise
> salt and pepper, to taste
>
> 10 leaves iceberg lettuce

Place salmon in bowl. Add hard-boiled eggs and stir gently to mix. Add all remaining ingredients except lettuce; stir gently. Place a couple of lettuce leaves on each plate and mound some salad in middle.

Starters: Salads

Avocado Shrimp Salad

(see photo p. 33)

Serves 4

You may have seen a terrible rumour out there on the Highway of Misinformation—also called the Internet—about a person who was eating shrimp and then drank a glass of orange juice containing vitamin C. The person suddenly began bleeding profusely and died. Apparently according to the autopsy report, the cause of death was believed to be a result of the arsenic compounds in the shrimp combined with the vitamin C. Well, I am here to say unequivocally that this story is nothing more than a fabricated rumour conjured up by someone's overactive imagination. Thank goodness too, since orange juice and shrimp are two wonders of nature and it would be a shame to never be allowed to enjoy them together.

1 lb (454 g) cooked medium to large shrimp, deveined
2 red peppers, seeded and finely chopped
2 avocados, peeled, pitted and chopped
3/4 tsp (4 mL) salt
1 tsp (5 mL) sugar
1/4 tsp (1 mL) pepper

8 to 10 leaves iceberg lettuce, torn into small pieces
1/2 cup (125 mL) Golden Italian dressing

In medium salad bowl, combine shrimp, red pepper, avocado, salt, sugar and pepper. Add lettuce. Pour dressing over salad, toss and serve.

Stuffed Arctic Char

(*see* photo p. 34)

Serves 4

Arctic char is a northern fish species that few people will ever see in the wild. It is a member of the trout family and tends to live exclusively above the 50th parallel in Canada's far north tributaries. Arctic char travels the cold northern rivers to spawn during late September and early fall, and it is considered to be the most northerly ranging member of the trout and salmon family. A land-locked variety of Arctic char may also be found in a handful of Québec lakes. This special char is known as Québec red trout and does not migrate.

1 Tbsp (15 mL) vegetable oil
1 small onion, sliced
1 × 1-inch (2.5 cm) piece ginger, julienned
1/2 small jalapeño pepper, thinly sliced

2 × 12 oz (340 g) whole Arctic char fillets, skin on
salt and pepper, to taste
6 lime leaves
several sprigs fresh cilantro
1 lime, thinly sliced

2 tsp (10 mL) vegetable oil, for brushing

Preheat grill to medium-high. In large skillet, heat oil. Add onion and cook until soft and golden brown. Add ginger and jalapeño pepper and sauté for 3 minutes more. Remove from heat.

Season char fillets with salt and pepper. Lay 1 fillet, flesh side up, on baking sheet. Arrange half of lime leaves and cilantro sprigs on top. Top with half of onion mix, spreading evenly. Top with lime slices and spread remaining onion mix on top of limes. Top with remaining lime leaves and cilantro and lay second fillet, skin side up, on top of filling, enclosing stuffing.

Tie fillets securely together with butcher's twine. Brush with oil and grill for about 4 to 5 minutes per side until middle of stuffing is hot when tested with a knife.

Arctic Char with Basil Sauce

(see photo p. 51)

Serves 2

The Québec red trout is a member of the Arctic char family veiled by myth and mystery and shrouded in secrecy. These special and unique "landlocked" Arctic char are found in only a small handful of lakes in Québec. Reds, as they are commonly called, are actually an old remnant population of Arctic char often confused with the brook trout in appearance and behaviour. The Québec red has a more sharply forked tail than the brook trout, is quite streamlined in shape and lacks the characteristic halo spots of the common brook trout. It is believed that several lakes in the province still hold sustaining populations of the landlocked char known as the Québec red, but very few people have ever seen them.

1/2 cup (125 mL) firmly packed fresh basil leaves
1/4 tsp (1 mL) minced garlic
1/8 tsp (0.5 mL) salt
3 1/2 Tbsp (52 mL) extra-virgin olive oil, *divided*

1/4 tsp (1 mL) packed light brown sugar
1 tsp (5 mL) red-wine vinegar
1 small tomato, cut into 1/4-inch (6 mm) slices
salt and pepper, to taste

1 × 8 to 10 oz (225 to 280 g) Arctic char fillet

Boil water in medium saucepan, and have a bowl of ice-cold water ready. Blanch basil leaves in boiling water for 15 to 20 seconds, then transfer quickly to cold water. Drain well, squeezing excess liquid from basil. Transfer basil to blender and purée with garlic, salt and 3 Tbsp (45 mL) oil. Set aside.

Preheat broiler. Line small broiler pan with foil. Grease foil or spray with non-stick cooking spray. In bowl, combine brown sugar and vinegar until sugar dissolves. Arrange tomato slices on platter or large plate; season to taste with salt and drizzle sugar mixture on top of tomato slices.

Coat char fillet with remaining 1/2 Tbsp (7 mL) oil and season with salt and pepper. Place fish on broiler pan. Broil for about 5 minutes until meat flakes easily with a fork. Arrange char on top of tomato slices and drizzle basil sauce over top. Serve immediately.

Bass Fillets with Béchamel

Serves 4

Cooking bass, as with cooking some other freshwater fish, may involve some tricks to mask their somewhat fishy taste. Although many bass species are not strong-flavoured *per se*, overall taste does depend on the individual fish. One trick for toning down any strong fishy taste is to first marinate the fish fillets for 2 to 4 hours. Excess oils and blood will leach out, which can increase palatability. Another technique is to soak the fillets in cooking wine for several hours. These marinating techniques are not limited to bass and may also be used on other strong or oily fish species.

> **4 bass fillets**
> **salt and pepper, to taste**
> **water**
>
> **2 Tbsp (30 mL) butter**
> **2 Tbsp (30 mL) flour**
> **pinch of freshly ground nutmeg**
> **1 1/2 cups (375 mL) cold milk**
> **1/4 cup (60 mL) sherry**

Place fillets in large skillet and season with salt and pepper. Cover fillets just barely with water and simmer until fish flakes easily.

Meanwhile, prepare Béchamel sauce: preheat broiler and melt butter in saucepan. Add flour and nutmeg; cook until flour browns, stirring constantly. Gradually add milk, stirring until well blended. Simmer until thickened. Add sherry, and then remove from heat altogether.

Transfer bass to baking dish and cover with sauce. Broil until sauce begins to turn brown. Serve with rice or potatoes (*see* Garlic Mashed Potatoes, p. 158).

 tip **MAKING BÉCHAMEL SAUCE**

Béchamel (or white sauce) is one of the "mother sauces" and is the basis of many recipes. A basic Béchamel sauce is quite easy. Heat 2 Tbsp (30 mL) butter in medium saucepan over low. Whisk in 2 Tbsp (30 mL) flour until smooth. Add 1 to 1 1/2 cups (250 to 375 mL) whole milk and continue whisking to remove lumps. Season with salt and pepper to taste.

Walnut-fried Bass

Serves 6

There are five species of bass in Canada, three of which are commonly found in most provinces. The smallmouth bass, largemouth bass and rock bass can be found in many lakes, rivers and streams in this country and are highly prized by professional and amateur anglers alike. Smallmouth and largemouth are the targets of North America's professional tournament fishing circuit. Bass are typically live-released in all of North America's bass fishing tournaments. Some anglers, however, target bass to eat, and they do make a good choice for many fish dishes. The meat is firm and white and best harvested early and late in the season when water temperatures are low. Bass are susceptible to black spot disease and white grub in warm-water conditions, but as unsightly as these parasites are, they are completely harmless to humans.

> **2 lbs (900 g) bass fillets**
> **pepper, to taste**
>
> **1 1/2 cups (375 mL) fresh breadcrumbs**
> **1 1/2 cups (375 mL) ground walnuts**
> **1 1/2 tsp (7 mL) crushed rosemary**
> **1/2 tsp (2 mL) thyme leaves**
>
> **1 cup (250 mL) flour**
> **2 eggs, beaten**
>
> **1/3 cup (75 mL) butter**
> **1/3 cup (75 mL) oil**

Season fillets with pepper. Combine breadcrumbs, walnuts, rosemary and thyme in bowl. Place flour on plate and beaten eggs in shallow bowl. Cover fillets with flour, dip in eggs, shaking off excess, and then roll in crumb mixture.

Heat butter and oil in skillet over medium. Place fish in skillet and fry for 5 minutes on each side until fish browns and flakes slightly with a fork. Place cooked fillets on paper towel–lined serving platter. Serve with Stovetop Capellini, p. 169.

Spicy Southern-style Bass

(*see* photo p. 52)

Serves 6

Bass are members of the sunfish family and are categorized as
a spiny-rayed, warm-water fish species. Bass spawn during the late spring
when water temperature reaches about 50°F (10°C). They prefer quiet,
shallow areas of lakes for spawning, usually less than 15 feet (4.6 metres) deep,
where they create an aquatic nest by clearing debris and mud from the
lake bottom. It is here they deposit their eggs, which they then guard until
hatching. Since bass tend to be one of the latest spring spawners, the bass
fishing season in Canada doesn't open until late June to allow bass the
opportunity to complete their reproductive cycle.

1/4 cup (60 mL) melted butter
1 small tomato, chopped
1/2 cup (125 mL) chopped onion
1/2 cup (125 mL) chopped green pepper
1/4 cup (60 mL) green chili salsa
3 Tbsp (45 mL) chopped black olives
1 Tbsp (15 mL) minced parsley
1 garlic clove, minced
hot pepper sauce, to taste

2 lbs (900 g) bass fillets

Preheat oven to 350°F (175°C). Mix butter, tomato, onion, green pepper,
salsa, olives, parsley, garlic and hot pepper sauce in large baking dish. Bake
for 10 minutes without fish, then add fish and drizzle sauce over top. Cover
and bake for another 20 minutes until fish flakes easily with a fork.

Bass with Leek Sauce

Serves 4

Across the Canadian Prairies, white-tailed deer are often referred to as "jumpers," named for their ability to leap 18 to 20 feet (5.5 to 6 metres) in a single bound. Although bass have never acquired that nickname, they could easily be called jumpers too. Both smallmouth and largemouth bass are known for leaping great distances out of the water when hooked. They often shake and thrash as they jump and, if the angler is not prepared, often will free themselves in the process. Fishermen call this "spitting the hook," but really it is slack line and the movement of the leaping bass that allows them to get away. I am aware of no other freshwater fish that leaps as consistently as the bass—our true Canadian jumper fish.

4 × 6 to 7 oz (170 to 200 g) bass fillets, skin on
salt and pepper

1 Tbsp (15 mL) + 1 tsp (5 mL) vegetable oil
2 shallots, peeled and minced
3 leeks (white part only), thinly sliced
1/2 cup (125 mL) chicken stock
juice from 1 lemon

2 Tbsp (30 mL) sliced fresh chives, for garnish

Preheat oven to 400°F (205°C). Season fillets with salt and pepper. Heat 1 Tbsp (15 mL) oil in large skillet over medium-high. Once oil begins to smoke, add fillets and sear until light golden brown. Transfer fillets to baking sheet and finish cooking in oven for about 7 minutes until just cooked through.

Meanwhile, reheat the same saucepan over medium-high. Add 1 tsp (5 mL) oil. Add shallots and leeks; cook, stirring, until translucent (do not brown). Add chicken stock, cover pan and simmer for about 15 minutes until leeks are very tender. Transfer mixture from saucepan to blender and purée until smooth. Drain through fine-mesh strainer if desired. Season with lemon juice, salt and pepper.

Serve bass fillets with leek sauce and garnish with chives.

Carp Casserole

Serves 4 to 6

Although the common carp is still considered an accidental exotic introduction into Canadian waters, we have learned how to adapt and live with it in Canada. There is, in fact, a growing interest in carp as a prized sport fish, and anglers are fishing for these large-scaled fish more than ever before. Yes, the common carp's image makeover did take some time, but most folks have finally resigned themselves to the fact that this fish has merit both as a sport fish and on the table.

3 cups (750 mL) cooked carp, broken into pieces
2 cups (500 mL) cooked rice
2 Tbsp (30 mL) grated onion
2 Tbsp (30 mL) melted better
1 Tbsp (15 mL) lemon juice
1/2 cup (125 mL) milk
2 beaten eggs
1 tsp (5 mL) salt

Preheat oven to 350°F (175°C). Combine all ingredients and place in greased baking pan. Bake for 50 minutes. Let stand 10 minutes before serving.

Try with This  **Baked Broccoli**

Serves 6

2 heads broccoli, cut into florets
2 tsp (10 mL) extra-virgin olive oil
1 tsp (5 mL) salt
1/2 tsp (2 mL) pepper
1 garlic clove, minced
1/2 tsp (2 mL) lemon juice

Preheat oven to 400°F (205°C). In large bowl, mix broccoli, oil, salt, pepper and garlic. Spread broccoli mixture out in one layer in shallow roasting pan or rimmed baking sheet. Bake for 15 to 20 minutes until broccoli stems are tender enough to pierce with a fork. Transfer to platter and squeeze lemon juice liberally over top; serve immediately.

Carp with Cilantro Butter

Serves 4

There is a small but dedicated group of carp fly enthusiasts in Canada who wouldn't give up their fish of choice for anything in the world. Since fly-fishermen generally focus on the lake or river surface to catch fish, they needed to adapt to the carp's bottom-feeding tendencies. With a few simple equipment modifications, anglers quickly learned how to entice carp with fly equipment and be successful at it.

> 1 cup (250 mL) softened butter
> 2 Tbsp (30 mL) chopped fresh cilantro
> 1 Tbsp (15 mL) chopped fresh parsley
> 1 shallot, finely chopped
> 2 tsp (10 mL) pepper
>
> 1 fresh whole carp, cleaned (*see* p. 5)

Mix butter, cilantro, parsley, shallot and pepper together in shallow bowl; refrigerate until solid.

Preheat oven to 375°F (190°C). Divide seasoned butter into 1/4-inch (6 mm) chunks. Place carp in foil roasting bag (or wrap well and seal in large sheet of foil) and top with cilantro butter pieces. Bake for 45 minutes. Serve hot.

Try with This  **Paprika-roasted Cauliflower**

Serves 4

1 × 3 lb (1.4 kg) head cauliflower, cut into florets
3 Tbsp (45 mL) olive oil
1/2 tsp (2 mL) paprika
1/4 tsp (1 mL) salt

Preheat oven to 400°F (205°C). In baking dish, combine florets, oil, paprika and salt and mix well. Cook, uncovered, for about 30 minutes, stirring once, until tender and slightly browned. Serve immediately.

Southern-fried Bullhead

Serves 6

Cooking your own fish is a labour of love that may at times bring difficulty, and cleaning catfish is one of those times. To properly prepare any type of catfish for the table, you will first need to complete the slightly unpleasant task of cutting and skinning your fish. Catfish are one of the few freshwater fish that require skinning rather than simply filleting or removing the scales. To make the job of skinning catfish easier, you will require a good set of pliers and a secure spot to anchor your fish. With some practice, the act of skinning catfish will become easier. What is waiting for you after the unpleasantness of preparation will more than make up for it!

> **peanut or sunflower oil, or lard**
> **1/4 cup (60 mL) cornmeal or seasoned breadcrumbs**
> **1/4 cup (60 mL) flour, seasoned with salt and pepper**
> **1 egg**
> **5 to 6 bullheads, skinned (*see* Tip), with head and tail removed**

In large, heavy saucepan, heat enough oil or lard to 375°F (190°C) to create a shallow fry, enough to cover fish. (Test oil temperature with kernel of corn; *see* p. 116) In shallow bowl, mix cornmeal and flour. In another shallow bowl, beat egg. Roll fish in flour mixture, then in egg, and back again in flour mixture. Fry for about 5 minutes until golden brown, turning only once. Drain on paper towel–lined plate before serving.

 tip   **SKINNING CATFISH**

> Skinning catfish is quite simple once you have done it a couple of times. For this task you will need a wood cutting board or fillet table, a pair of pliers, a dry towel and a sharp fillet knife. Start by cutting through the fish's skin just below the head, and cut the skin through 360° around the fish. With a dry towel in your right hand, hold onto the head tightly, and then grab the edge of the fish's skin tightly with the pliers. Pull slowly with your left hand and the skin should peel away much like a sausage casing. Stop when you get to the tail and cut the skin away completely with the fillet knife. Rinse the fish off in cold water and you're all set!

Catfish with Corn and Black Bean Salsa

Serves 6

Jac Eckhardt, head chef at Toronto's famous Zee Grill Restaurant and Oyster Bar, believes the garnish served with any fish is 60 percent of a successful dish. When cooking any bland-tasting fish, Eckhardt says, you'll need to add more than just salt and pepper. One treatment he uses is a thin crust of mashed sweet potato mixed with butter, cinnamon and a touch of aged Cheddar. Broiling this dish caramelizes the crust and gives the fish an attitude it may not deserve—but it certainly makes it delicious! The Corn and Black Bean Salsa presented here adds a unique attitude to this catfish recipe.

2 ears corn, husked

1 cup (250 mL) black beans
1/2 cup (125 mL) tomatoes, peeled, seeded and diced
1 small jalapeño pepper, seeded and chopped
1 cucumber, chopped
1/3 cup (75 mL) minced red onion
1/3 cup (75 mL) diced red pepper
1/4 cup (60 mL) lime juice
salt and pepper, to taste

1/4 cup (60 mL) olive oil
6 × 5 to 6 oz (140 to 170 g) catfish fillets
1/2 cup (125 mL) milk
1 cup (250 mL) breadcrumbs

Preheat grill to medium. Grill corn, turning often, until slightly charred. Let cool and then remove kernels from both cobs.

To make salsa, combine corn kernels with black beans, tomatoes, jalapeño, cucumber, red onion, red pepper and lime juice in mixing bowl. Season with salt and pepper; set aside.

Preheat oven to 400°F (205°C). Heat oil in large skillet over medium-high until barely smoking. Sprinkle fillets with salt and pepper. Place milk and breadcrumbs in separate shallow plates. Dip fillets in milk and roll in breadcrumbs, then sauté until golden brown. Move catfish fillets to rimmed baking sheet and bake for 5 minutes. Serve with salsa.

Catfish Tacos

(see photo p. 69)

Serves 4

Catfish anglers are a different breed of fishermen. Since most species of catfish found in Canada are nocturnal feeders, most catfishing occurs after dark. The whiskered catfish, whether channel cats or bullheads, provide a great challenge to those who try to catch them. They are mostly benthic (bottom-feeders), so the most popular way to catch catfish is by still or drift fishing. Catfish bait choice is extensive and wide-ranging and includes worm balls, hot dogs and even chicken livers. So long as the bait remains still and near the bottom, resident catfish will locate it with the help of their barbells. Once a catfish is hooked, it will fight like the dickens, giving anglers a real run for their money!

1 Tbsp (15 mL) oil
1 tsp (5 mL) chili powder
1/2 tsp (2 mL) dried oregano
1/4 tsp (1 mL) salt
1/4 tsp (1 mL) pepper
1 lb (454 g) catfish fillets

1/2 cup (125 mL) shredded carrot
1/4 cup (60 mL) diced red onion
1 tsp (5 mL) fresh lime juice

1/4 cup (60 mL) plain yogurt or sour cream
1 Tbsp (15 mL) minced fresh cilantro
1 green onion, minced

8 small flour or corn tortillas
1 small tomato, diced
1 avocado, peeled and diced

Preheat grill to medium-high and coat with non-stick cooking spray.
On plate, combine oil, chili powder, oregano, salt and pepper. Coat fish fillets in mixture. Grill fillets with lid down for about 5 minutes, turning once, until fish flakes easily.

While catfish cooks, combine carrot, red onion and lime juice in bowl.
In separate bowl, combine yogurt, cilantro and green onion.

Break fish into chunks and divide among tortillas on individual plates.
Top with yogurt mixture, carrot mixture, tomato and avocado, and serve.

Avocado Shrimp Salad (p. 21)

Stuffed Arctic Char (p. 22)

Catfish Court-Bouillon

Serves 4

Our most common member of the whiskered fish family, the channel catfish, is one heck of a challenging fish to catch. Canadian "catfisherfolk" use a variety of techniques for catching catfish consistently. The key to enticing a catfish into striking is to present your bait on or near the bottom of the lake or river. Channel cats use their whiskers to sense and locate food and may travel large areas in search of a snack. "Still fishing" has proven to be the best way to trigger a strike. Offerings such as a worm ball, dead minnows or even a chunk of beef liver will do the trick. Anglers wait for the slightest movement in their line—signalling that a cat has picked it up—before setting the hook.

> 2 lbs (900 g) catfish fillets, skin removed (*see* Tip, p. 30)
>   and flesh cut into large chunks
> 1 1/2 tsp (7 mL) salt
> 1 tsp (5 mL) pepper
> 1 tsp (5 mL) red pepper flakes
> 1 yellow onion, finely chopped
> 1 cup (250 mL) chopped green onions
> 1/3 cup (75 mL) flour
> 1/2 cup (125 mL) cooking oil
> 1 × 8 oz (227 mL) can tomato sauce
> 1 cup (250 mL) water

Place all ingredients in a heavy pot, mix gently and cover. Simmer over medium for about 10 minutes, occasionally gently shaking pot instead of stirring (which will cause the fish to break up). Cook for 10 minutes more until fish flakes easily when tested with a fork. Serve with rice.

Catfish Sandwich

Serves 4

Catfish can be caught in a variety of ways but none are as strange or as dangerous as a method known as "noddling." Noddling is a technique for catching these whiskered giants using nothing but your bare hands. The angler wades into the murky catfish water, moving his hands in and out of holes and stumps at the bottom, searching for possible catfish hiding places. Once he has located a catfish hole, the noddler allows the cat to latch onto his hand and he must then wrestle the fish to the surface. Since catfish do not possess sharp teeth, the angler usually will not be seriously injured by a bite. The problem, however, is the size and strength of catfish—people in the United States have died while noddling. For the most part, noddling is not an angling style of great popularity in Canada.

> 4 × 6 to 8 oz (170 to 225 g) catfish fillets
> 1 Tbsp (15 mL) peanut or canola oil
> 1/4 tsp (1 mL) salt
> 1/4 tsp (1 mL) pepper
>
> 1/4 cup (60 mL) mayonnaise
> 2 tsp (10 mL) lemon juice
> 1 garlic clove, minced
> 1/4 tsp (1 mL) Worcestershire sauce
> 1/4 tsp (1 mL) hot pepper sauce
>
> 4 egg buns, cut in half
> 4 leaves iceberg lettuce

Preheat grill to medium and spray grill with non-stick spray or coat with oil. Brush fillets with oil and season with salt and pepper. Grill fillets until fish flakes easily when tested with a fork and outside is golden brown.

In mixing bowl, combine mayonnaise, lemon juice, garlic, Worcestershire sauce and hot pepper sauce. Spread mixture on both halves of each bun. Place cooked fillets and lettuce leaves on bun bottoms. Cover with top halves and serve.

Kids' Fish Sticks

Serves 4

According to government statistics, Canada is the world's seventh-largest exporter of fish and seafood products, with exports going to more than 130 countries. The United States is Canada's largest export market and represents roughly 62 percent of our seafood trade, followed by the European Union (15 percent), Japan (8 percent) and China (6 percent).

> 1 cup (250 mL) flour
> 1/4 cup (60 mL) cornmeal
> 1 tsp (5 mL) baking powder
> 1 tsp (5 mL) Cajun seasoning
> 1 tsp (5 mL) parsley
> 1 tsp (5 mL) salt
> 1/2 tsp (2 mL) pepper
> 1/2 cup (125 mL) buttermilk
> 1 egg, beaten
> 4 × 6 to 8 oz (170 to 225 g) cod or halibut fillets, cut into strips
>
> 1 1/2 cups (375 mL) olive oil

In bowl, mix flour, cornmeal, baking powder, Cajun seasoning, parsley, salt and pepper. In second bowl, combine buttermilk and egg. Toss fish pieces in flour mixture, then in buttermilk mixture, then again in flour mixture.

Heat oil in large skillet to about 325°F (160°C). Gently place fish pieces in hot oil and fry for 6 to 8 minutes, turning every 2 minutes, until golden brown. Drain on paper towels; sprinkle with salt. Serve with ketchup or Homemade Tartar Sauce (below).

Try with This

Homemade Tartar Sauce

Serves 4

1 cup (250 mL) mayonnaise
1/3 cup (75 mL) sweet pickle relish
1 Tbsp (15 mL) minced capers
1 hard-boiled egg, peeled and chopped
1/2 tsp (2 mL) Worcestershire sauce
1/2 tsp (2 mL) salt
1/2 tsp (2 mL) pepper

In small bowl, combine mayonnaise, relish, capers and egg. Mix well and add Worcestershire sauce, salt and pepper. Stir and refrigerate before serving.

Indian Cod with Noodles

Serves 4

Long before codfish stocks became the subject of great controversy in this country, English, French, Spanish and Portuguese fishermen flocked to Newfoundland and the Grand Banks to fish for this highly prized fish. Early settlers to North America not only consumed codfish extensively, but they exported it to Europe and the Caribbean. In the 1800s as the West was being settled, salt cod was a cheap food alternative for Western workers and navigators. Codfish from Newfoundland even found its way into the Deep South of the United States as a food source for slaves. Over 200 years later, codfish is still an important source of food and provides employment for many Newfoundlanders.

2 Tbsp (30 mL) vegetable oil
1 large onion, chopped
2 garlic cloves, chopped
6 Tbsp (90 mL) finely chopped mushrooms
8 oz (225 g) cod fillets, cut into 1-inch (2.5 cm) cubes
2 Tbsp (30 mL) red curry paste
1 3/4 cups (425 mL) coconut milk
1 tsp (5 mL) brown sugar
1 tsp (5 mL) Thai fish sauce
handful of chopped fresh cilantro, *divided*

4 oz (115 g) package of dried rice noodles
3 scallions (or shallots), chopped
1/2 cup (125 mL) bean sprouts
handful of fresh Thai basil leaves

In large skillet or wok, heat oil over medium. Add onion, garlic and mushrooms and cook, stirring frequently, until softened but not browned. Add fish cubes, curry paste and coconut milk; bring to a gentle boil. Let simmer for 2 to 3 minutes, then add sugar, fish sauce and 1/2 of cilantro. Keep warm.

Prepare noodles according to package directions. Drain well in metal strainer, then add scallions, bean sprouts and most of basil to strainer. Place over pot of hot water. Steam for 1 to 2 minutes; drain thoroughly and transfer to serving dish. Top with fish curry; sprinkle remaining cilantro and basil over top.

 tip   Ingredients for this recipe should be easily found in most grocery stores; if not, ask for them at an Asian grocery.

Newfoundland Cod au Gratin

Serves 10

Newfoundland cod are a unique and powerful fish. While fishing for cod in Seal Cove back in the 1980s, I was amazed by the strength and stamina of this magnificent fish. Much of the cod fishing at the time was done using a monofilament hand-line used in a jigging manner. Depending on the size of fish, sometimes it took all my strength to pull a large cod up from 60 feet (18 metres) below. I was just a teenager at the time, but will never forget the determined look on the cods' faces as they neared the boat. My host made it look easy, but as a scrawny teenage boy, it was all I could do just to get a chunky cod up over the gunnels.

> 1/2 cup (125 mL) salt
> 8 cups (2 L) water
> 4 lbs (1.8 kg) cod fillets
>
> 3 cups (750 mL) milk
> 1/2 cup (125 mL) butter
> 1/2 cup (125 mL) flour
>
> 2 Tbsp (30 mL) grated Parmesan cheese
> 1 1/4 cups (300 mL) grated old Cheddar cheese
> paprika, for sprinkling

In large pot, make brine by dissolving salt in water. Simmer cod for 10 minutes in brine; drain. Transfer fish to large bowl and set aside. Place milk in double boiler over high. In medium skillet over medium, melt butter. Add flour and cook until bubbly. Set aside.

Preheat broiler. When milk is hot, add flour mixture and stir until lumps disappear. Transfer to large bowl with fish; stir gently so as not to break up fish too much. Divide into 10 ovenproof ramekins; sprinkle with cheeses and paprika. Broil until brown on top.

Steamed Salt Cod

Serves 4

No Canadian fish has been discussed and debated so intensely as the Atlantic cod. Following a moratorium on cod in 1992, fishing for this once hugely important fish species has been sporadic. Codfish population decline, resulting from climate change, overfishing and predation from seals, has placed this species in some turmoil. There is, however, some evidence to show that cod populations may be on the rise again. It is unlikely that they will ever reach the heights they were at 20 to 25 years ago, when landings reached 400,000 tonnes and more. Nevertheless, fishing for cod does continue unabated in certain areas of Atlantic Canada, where it remains an important source of food and livelihood.

> 2 × 10 oz (280 g) cod fillets
> salt
>
> 3 slices ginger
> 1 spring onion, chopped
> 1/2 tsp (2 mL) chili powder
> pepper, to taste
> 2 tomatoes, quartered

Place fillets in large electric food steamer (*see* Tip). Sprinkle with enough salt to cover completely; set aside for 30 minutes. Mix ginger, onion, chili powder and pepper and sprinkle over cod fillets. Arrange tomato quarters around steamer. Steam for 10 to 15 minutes. Serve right out of steamer.

 tip   There are a variety of electric vegetable or rice steamers on the market, and they all work well for this recipe.

Cod Fish Tacos

Serves 4

We all know the health benefits of eating fish regularly, but getting the kids to share the enthusiasm can sometimes be a daunting task. The perfect way to keep the youngsters happy is giving a new spin to an old recipe and involving fish in some way, as with these fish tacos. A basic fish fillet dish may not seem all that enticing to young people, so ensuring that the food remains new and exciting is the key. The same holds true for introducing youth to the pastime of sport fishing itself. Keep things new and interesting and you will find a way to pique their curiosity.

1/4 tsp (1 mL) ground cumin
1/4 tsp (1 mL) dried oregano
1 lb (454 g) cod or halibut fillets
1 Tbsp (15 mL) olive oil
1 lime

12 corn tortillas

1/3 cup (75 mL) sour cream
2 cups (500 mL) shredded cabbage
1 cup (250 mL) salsa

Combine cumin and oregano in bowl and spread evenly over both sides of fish. Drizzle with oil and a squeeze of lime.

On one burner, preheat skillet over medium, and on another burner, preheat grill pan over medium-low. Warm tortillas one at a time in skillet until flexible; set aside.

Turn up heat on grill pan to medium-high, then add fish and cook until golden brown, turning once. Cut cooked fish into small pieces and set aside. Add sour cream to each warm tortilla shell and divide fish up on top of sour cream. Top with shredded cabbage and a spoonful of salsa. Serve immediately.

Cod Curry

Serves 8

For many people, one of the somewhat unpleasant aspects of fishing is trying to scrub away the fishy smell afterward. One trick you can use to rid yourself of that lingering fishy smell is to first wash your hands thoroughly with a floral-scented dish soap and rinse completely. Then pour 2 to 3 ounces (60 to 85 millilitres) dental mouthwash into your hands and rub it in as if you were washing your hands with soap; it will completely mask any fish smell. If one soaking of mouthwash doesn't do the trick, wash again with dish soap and repeat the mouthwash bath. You will be amazed how well it works.

1 × 2-inch (5 cm) piece ginger, chopped
4 bay leaves, *divided*
7 red chili peppers, *divided*
5 tsp (25 mL) + pinch of mustard seed
1 Tbsp (15 mL) + pinch of cumin seed

2 lbs (900 g) cod fillets
2 tsp (10 mL) salt
2 Tbsp (30 mL) garlic powder
3 tsp (15 mL) turmeric, *divided*

1 cup (250 mL) + 3 Tbsp (45 mL) canola or peanut oil, *divided*
4 shallots, chopped
2 tomatoes, diced

3 cups (750 mL) water
juice from 1/2 lemon

Place ginger, 2 bay leaves, 5 red chili peppers, mustard seed and cumin seed in bowl of blender or grinder; pulse until powdered. Slice fish into 2- to 3-inch (5 to 7.5 cm) chunks and place on large plate. Drizzle with salt, garlic powder and 2 tsp (10 mL) turmeric. Rub fish with spicy powder from blender; set aside for 1/2 hour.

Heat 1 cup (250 mL) oil in large skillet and fry fish a few pieces at a time until done. Set cooked fish aside. Clean skillet then add 3 Tbsp (45 mL) fresh oil and heat. Add pinch of mustard seed, pinch of cumin seed, 2 red chili peppers, 2 bay leaves and chopped shallots. Cook, stirring, until browned slightly; add tomatoes and 1 tsp (5 mL) turmeric. Stir and cook until slightly browned.

Add water and bring to a boil. Add fish and cook for 12 minutes. Remove from heat and add lemon juice. Serve immediately.

Fried Salt Cod with Island Sauce

Serves 4

Salt cod is to Newfoundland what apple pie is to the United States. It is and always has been a staple food for those who live on the Rock. Often served with such Newfoundland oddities as pease pudding, Jigg's dinner or Purity hard tack, the traditional Newfoundland salt cod was originally an invention of necessity. Since proper cooling was not always available on the island, and root cellars far outnumbered refrigerators, salted cod was made to last a long time without spoiling. Even after the arrival of modern conveniences to the island, Newfies continue to eat and enjoy salt cod.

> 1 lb (454 g) salt cod
>
> 1/2 lb (225 g) potatoes, peeled and
>   cut into 1- to 2- inch (2.5 to 5 cm) chunks
> 2 eggs
> 1/4 cup (60 mL) flour
> 2 shallots, chopped
> salt and pepper, to taste
>
> 1 cup (250 mL) oil, for frying
>
> 1 cup (250 mL) mayonnaise
> 1 Tbsp (15 mL) lemon juice
> 1 Tbsp (15 mL) chopped capers

Soak salt cod in fresh water for 1 day. Drain cod, remove excess water and break apart into small pieces.

Boil potatoes until soft. Mash potatoes and stir in cod. Whisk eggs in mixing bowl. Add flour and shallots, stirring well. Add potato-cod mixture; stir to combine. Season with salt and pepper.

Heat 1 to 2 inches (2.5 to 5 cm) oil in steep-sided skillet or cast-iron pan. Place cod mixture in spoonfuls in oil and fry until golden brown. Turn once. Drain on paper towel.

Whisk mayonnaise, lemon juice and capers together in small mixing bowl. Season with salt and pepper. Serve cod with lemon mayonnaise.

Cod Soufflé

Serves 4

Newfoundlanders have, in recent years, enjoyed more liberal recreational fishing for cod in their province. Thanks to an announcement by Gail Shea, Canada's Minister of Fisheries and Oceans, for three weeks each summer and one week in the fall, residents are permitted to fish recreationally for cod. The province's daily cod bag limit remains at five fish; however, a new "boat limit" of 15 fish was put in place when three or more people are fishing. Recreational cod fishing is a tradition most islanders have grown up with and the ability to cast line in their spare time is something they take seriously. Cod is not only a staple fish of Newfoundland; it is a huge part of eastern culture and heritage.

> 2 Tbsp (30 mL) butter
> 2 Tbsp (30 mL) flour
> 1/2 cup (125 mL) milk
> 8 oz (225 g) cooked cod, flaked
> 4 egg whites
> 2 Tbsp (30 mL) cream (18%)
> salt and pepper, to taste

Preheat oven to 400°F (205°C). Heat butter and flour in large saucepan and gradually stir in milk. Bring to a boil and simmer until mixture thickens. Mix in fish, egg whites, cream and salt and pepper.

Put in soufflé dish, filling to about 1/4 full. Tie buttered paper around dish so it extends above top. Bake for about 30 minutes.

Try with This 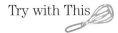 **Roasted Asparagus**

Serves 4

1 lb (454 g) asparagus, tough stems snapped off and discarded
1 Tbsp (15 mL) olive oil
1 tsp (5 mL) salt
1 Tbsp (15 mL) balsamic vinegar

Preheat oven to 400°F (205°C). Place asparagus spears in shallow roasting pan. Drizzle with oil and sprinkle with salt, shaking pan and rolling spears around so that they are evenly coated. Roast for 10 to 15 minutes. Transfer to small platter and drizzle with balsamic vinegar. Serve immediately.

 tip

For a great appetizer, roll a thin slice of prosciutto or pancetta around each spear before roasting as above.

Cod Cakes

Serves 6

Of all the oddities served on the island of Newfoundland, fish cakes are definitely the most popular. They are to Newfoundland what poutine is to Québec or coffee is to Vancouver. Yes, Newfies do love their fish, it's true, but they simply adore their fish cakes! It does not matter whether you live in Corner Brook or Come By Chance or happen to be a townie and live in St. John's, the fish cake is an island staple, and "by gad boy" you're not a true Newfoundlander if you haven't eaten one!

> **4 oz (115 g) salt pork**
> **2 lbs (900 g) salt cod**
>
> **1 onion, diced**
> **8 potatoes, boiled and mashed**
> **1 cup (250 mL) flour**

Cut salt pork into small pieces and cook in medium skillet over medium. Remove pork, leaving drippings in skillet, and remove skillet from heat. Use pork in another recipe.

Cook salt cod in pan in boiling water for 15 minutes, then drain off water completely and allow cod to cool.

Break cod into small chunks and mix with onion and potatoes together in large bowl. Place flour in shallow bowl. Mould fish and potato mixture into small cake shapes and roll gently in flour. Return skillet to medium and fry cakes in pork drippings until golden brown on both sides.

Try with This 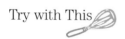 **Vegetable Rice**

(*see* photo p. 106)

Serves 4

1 cup (250 mL) uncooked long-grain rice
2 1/4 cups (550 mL) water
2 Tbsp (30 mL) onion (or vegetable) soup mix
1/4 tsp (1 mL) salt
2 cups (500 mL) frozen corn, peas or mixed vegetables

In saucepan, combine rice, water, soup mix and salt and bring to a boil. Add vegetables and return to a boil. Reduce heat; cover and simmer for about 15 minutes until rice and vegetables are tender.

Canadian Cod Cheeks

Serves 4

Everyone knows the best cut of pork or beef is the filet mignon or tenderloin, but did you know the best part of a fish is its cheeks? Yes, the cheeks of any fish are considered to be the superior-tasting meat; they are the filet mignon of the water world. The problem with most Canadian fish, however, is the cheek size and difficulty in removing them. In larger species like cod or halibut, the cheeks are considerably larger, making them easier to remove. That might explain the popularity of fish cheeks in many parts of the Maritimes, where they are served more frequently than in other parts of the country. Trust me, if you've never tried fish cheeks, you don't know what you are missing!

> 2 Tbsp (30 mL) butter
> 1 onion, diced
> 2 garlic cloves, minced
> 1 tsp (5 mL) salt
> 1/2 tsp (2 mL) lemon juice
> 1 tsp (5 mL) dill
> 1/4 cup (60 mL) white wine
>
> 1 lb (454 g) cod cheeks

Mix all ingredients except fish together in medium saucepan. Cook on medium-high until liquid reduces to mushy paste.

Preheat grill to medium. Cut 12-inch (30 cm) sections of foil and place 4 to 5 cheeks on each. Spread onion mix thoroughly over cod cheeks and seal foil around fish by folding edges to create small packets. Repeat until all cod cheeks are covered with mix and packed into small foil packets. Grill packets for 10 to 12 minutes, turning several times, until cheeks are opaque. Serve hot.

Cod Fish Stew

Serves 4

While camping in Prince Edward Island in 1995, my wife and I enjoyed some of the best cod fishing and eating I have ever experienced. During an afternoon of charter boat fishing off the Island's north shore, Cheryl and I hooked into and landed no less than eight nice-sized codfish. There are two things I will never forget from that day: one was how the big boat rocked back and forth in the 4- to 5-foot (1.2- to 1.5-metre) waves, and the other was the look on my wife's face as she hooked into those big cod—it was priceless! Cheryl and I gorged ourselves on awesome fish following that adventure. I tell you, there is nothing as tasty as fresh cod, and nothing as fulfilling as enjoying fish you caught with your own two hands!

> 1/4 cup (60 mL) soybean oil
> 2 medium onions, finely chopped
> 4 green onions, finely chopped
> 2 fresh red chili peppers, finely chopped
>
> 4 cups (1 L) half-and-half cream
> 1 lb (454 g) cod fillets, cut into 1-inch (2.5 cm) cubes
> salt and pepper, to taste

Heat oil in saucepan over medium. Stir in onions, green onions and red chili peppers. Cook and stir for about 5 minutes until onions are tender.

Blend cream into mixture, and simmer until thickened. Mix in cod cubes and cook until fish flakes easily with a fork. Season with salt and pepper, and serve in warmed bowls.

Pan-fried Eel

Serves 4

The American eel tends to strike fear in most people, and unjustly so. The eel's long, cylindrical body and snake-like head have, unfortunately, become the stuff of nightmares to many. Eels are a misunderstood and gentle fish with a life cycle and population now in some peril. As one of Canada's few catadromous spawners—fish that travel to salt water to spawn—the eel is unique in how far it travels each year to keep its numbers strong. Migration barriers such as dams are the eel's worst enemy because they prevent natural spawning behaviour. The eel has overcome many obstacles and remains one of the most unique wild fish species in Canada.

3 Tbsp (45 mL) olive oil
1/2 garlic clove
1 lb (454 g) eel, sliced into 2-inch (5 cm) pieces
salt and pepper, to taste

4 slices ginger
8 mushrooms, sliced
2 onions, sliced
1 cup (250 mL) water

Heat oil and garlic in cast-iron pan. Season eel slices with salt and pepper. Add eel slices to pan and sauté until golden brown. Transfer to saucepan and add ginger, mushrooms, onions and water. Bring to a boil, cover and simmer for 10 to 15 minutes. Serve hot.

Try with This  ## Sweet Scalloped Potatoes

Serves 4

1 × 13 oz (370 mL) can evaporated milk
2 tsp (10 mL) chicken bouillon
1 tsp (5 mL) onion powder
4 cups (1 L) sweet potatoes, peeled and sliced

In large skillet over medium-high, heat milk, bouillon and onion powder, stirring, until smooth. Add sweet potatoes and bring to a boil. Cover and let simmer for 30 minutes, stirring occasionally, until sauce has thickened and potatoes are soft.

Halibut on the Grill

Serves 4

Because of their mammoth size, Pacific halibut are fish to be reckoned with. They are the largest flatfish in the world, capable of reaching staggering weights of between 550 and 660 pounds (250 and 300 kilograms). Halibut are highly sought after by sport anglers off the coastal waters of British Columbia for their sporting quality and their taste. The International Pacific Halibut Commission, an organization established by the United States and Canada in 1923, has worked toward managing and conserving halibut waters shared by both countries. These fish grow extremely quickly and live a long time. Many specimen caught by fishermen have reached 20-plus years, and one geezer halibut was even recorded at 55 years old.

> oil, for brushing foil
> 1 lb (454 g) baby potatoes, quartered
> 1 lb (454 g) asparagus, rinsed well and tough ends snapped off
> 1 onion, sliced
> 1/2 lb (225 g) cherry tomatoes
> 4 halibut fillets
> fresh herbs, any kind
> 1 cup (250 mL) red-wine vinaigrette dressing, *divided*

Establish good bed of campfire coals or preheat barbecue to medium-high, or 350°F (175°C). Cut off 4 sheets of foil and brush with oil. Divide vegetables among foil sheets and place halibut on top; drizzle each pile with your choice of fresh herbs and 1/4 cup (60 mL) red-wine vinaigrette. Join corners of each foil square to seal tightly and place packages on grill. Cook until fish begins to flake; serve hot.

Nutty Campfire Halibut

Serves 4

According to experts, halibut are some of the mildest, most pleasant-tasting fish available on the market today. Halibut fillets do not contain an overabundance of oil, which can be both good and bad from a cooking standpoint. "Low-oil fish" usually have a mild, pleasant taste, but, depending on the style of dish, that can also mean they will stick to the pan. Be mindful of this when preparing any white meat fish with low oil content. Since these fish are so mild, some people prefer the use of a good marinade to spruce up the taste before preparing the dish. Others find that brushing the fillets with a generous amount of melted butter helps in that regard.

2 lbs (900 g) halibut fillets
3 Tbsp (45 mL) melted butter
1/4 cup (125 mL) shelled and finely chopped pistachio nuts

Prepare campfire or preheat barbecue to medium. Coat each fillet with melted butter, and then roll gently in chopped nuts. Cook halibut for 10 to 12 minutes, turning once halfway through. Fish will be firm and opaque when fully cooked. Remove fish carefully from grill and place gently on platter. Serve hot with rice or mixed vegetables (*see* Basmati Rice, p. 163, or Paprika-roasted Cauliflower, p. 29).

Try with This  **Kiwi Dip**

Makes 2 cups (500 mL)

3 kiwis, peeled and diced
2 medium tangerines or clementines, peeled and diced
1/2 cup (125 mL) diced red pepper
1/4 cup (60 mL) chopped cilantro
1 Tbsp (15 mL) lime juice
1 Tbsp (15 mL) vegetable oil
1/3 tsp (1.5 mL) salt

Combine ingredients in large bowl, mixing well. Refrigerate before serving. Makes great dipping sauce for many fried fish recipes.

Arctic Char with Basil Sauce (p. 23)

Spicy Southern-style Bass (p. 26)

Halibut Lasagna

Serves 8

The Atlantic halibut population has been devastated by the effects of overfishing and was placed on the endangered species list in 1996. Now a member of the dreaded "red list," the Atlantic halibut are at risk of extinction. As concerned citizens, we should avoid eating Atlantic halibut whenever possible and ensure the halibut we eat are from Pacific waters. Nearly all halibut sold in Canada are from the Pacific Northwest, where populations continue to be strong.

3 Tbsp (45 mL) butter
2 Tbsp (30 mL) flour
2 cups (500 mL) milk
2 Tbsp (30 mL) lemon juice
1 tsp (5 mL) nutmeg
1 tsp (5 mL) dry mustard
1 cup (250 mL) sour cream
1 cup (250 mL) shredded Cheddar cheese

2 Tbsp (30 mL) olive oil
1 onion, chopped
2 Tbsp (30 mL) minced garlic
1/2 tsp (2 mL) dried basil
2 eggs, beaten
1 × 15 oz (425 g) tub ricotta cheese or cottage cheese

12 cooked lasagna noodles
2 lbs (900 g) halibut, cooked and crumbled
1 cup (250 mL) shredded mozzarella cheese
1/4 cup (60 mL) Parmesan cheese

Heat butter in medium saucepan. Stir in flour, then milk, and cook until bubbly, stirring often. Reduce heat and whisk in lemon juice, nutmeg and mustard. Add sour cream and Cheddar cheese, and cook until cheese melts. Set aside.

Heat oil in medium skillet and sauté onion and garlic. Add basil and remove from heat. While cooling, mix in eggs and ricotta cheese.

Preheat oven to 375°F (190°C). In large casserole dish, layer a third of sauce, then 4 noodles, then half of ricotta mixture and half of fish. Repeat, and then finish with remaining pasta, Cheddar cheese sauce, mozzarella and Parmesan. Bake for about 30 minutes. Let stand for 5 minutes before serving.

Halibut Ceviche

Serves 4

The Pacific halibut is the largest of the flatfish family; its enormous size is its most distinguishing characteristic. The Latin name for Pacific halibut refers to its gargantuan girth and translates as "Hippo of the Sea." The English name is derived from "holy flatfish"—"hali" for holy and "but" for flat—because it was a special fish served on holy days or "holidays" in Medieval England. Pacific halibut has been harvested in North America since the 1880s.

> **2 lbs (900 g) very fresh halibut fillets,**
>   **cut into 1/2-inch (1.25 cm) cubes (*see* Tip)**
> **2 jalapeño peppers, seeded and finely chopped**
> **juice from 2 limes**
> **1/2 cup (125 mL) diced red onion**
> **1/4 cup (60 mL) vegetable cocktail or tomato juice**
> **salt and pepper, to taste**

Gently mix ingredients together in large bowl. Refrigerate overnight. Remove from refrigerator just before serving; do not let it sit for any length of time outside of fridge.

 tip   Ceviche is a method of preparation thought to originate in South America. The fish is marinated in a citrus and tomato mixture until it is "cooked." The fish is not cooked over heat, so it must be very fresh. In South America, ceviche might be served with anything from sweet potato slices to chips and popcorn. For this Halibut Ceviche, I suggest chips and fresh salsa or guacamole, and cold beer.

Baked Halibut

Serves 4

Many anglers who venture to British Columbia in search of salmon undoubtedly run into the reigning king of the West Coast, the mighty Pacific halibut. Salmon charter boats along the coast all the way up to Haida Gwaii and north include both halibut and salmon as their main target species. Sure, king salmon in excess of 50 pounds (23 kilograms) are caught with some regularity, but what about a specimen that can weigh as much as the angler and perhaps more? Just imagine hooking into a fish powerful enough to move the entire boat and easily capable of pulling a fisherman overboard. Halibut fishing, as with other large deep-sea fishing, is serious business. Anglers are strapped into fighting chairs and are linked to their rod and reel with a heavy strap and chain. There is no messing around when it comes to halibut.

3 shallots, chopped, *divided*
2 lbs (900 g) halibut fillets, thinly sliced
salt and pepper, to taste
1/2 cup (125 mL) cornmeal
1 Tbsp (15 mL) chopped parsley
1/4 cup (60 mL) half-and-half cream
1/4 cup (60 mL) white wine
3 Tbsp (45 mL) butter, melted

Preheat oven to 375°F (190°C). Grease shallow baking dish and sprinkle with half of shallots. Season fish lightly on both sides with salt and pepper and roll up. Sprinkle with remaining shallots, cornmeal and chopped parsley. Pour cream and white wine slowly over fish. Drizzle butter over fish. Bake for 30 minutes. Allow to sit for 5 minutes before serving.

Baked Halibut with Wild Garlic

Serves 4

With any fish recipe that calls for onions, such as this one, try sprucing things up a tad by substituting wild garlic. Wild garlic, or wild leeks as some folks call them, are one of nature's most perfect foods. My family harvests our own wild garlic each spring in May, a time my daughters and I look forward to all year long. The bulbs of the wild garlic plant may be pickled or eaten fresh, and the leaves of the plant make a great addition to any tossed salad. When used with fish, the wild garlic bulbs offer a unique and pleasant aroma and taste to your dish. Be sure to practise conservation when picking these magnificent plants because they are protected in provinces such as Québec, where harvest numbers are limited to just a few plants per person.

> 1/2 Tbsp (7 mL) olive oil
> 1/2 cup (125 mL) diced red pepper
> 1/4 cup (60 mL) diced red onion (or wild garlic bulbs)
> 1/4 cup (60 mL) chopped green olives
>
> 4 halibut fillets
> salt and pepper, to taste
> 2 Tbsp (30 mL) mayonnaise

Preheat oven to 400°F (205°C). Spray medium casserole dish with non-stick cooking spray and set aside. Heat olive oil in skillet and sauté red pepper, onion (or wild garlic bulbs) and olives for about 4 minutes. Set aside.

Season halibut fillets with salt and pepper and place in casserole dish. Spread mayonnaise over each fish, completely covering. Spread pepper mixture over top of fish. Bake for 15 to 20 minutes until fish is golden brown and flakes easily with a fork. Let stand 5 minutes before serving.

Stuffed Halibut

Serves 4 to 6

The Pacific halibut is an extremely important fish for the Canadian and American fishing industries. On the West Coast, halibut are caught with hook and line and brought to market, in some cases selling for more than $5 per pound ($2.25 per kilogram). Around Vancouver Island and up to Alaska, the halibut lurk in offshore reaches of the Pacific Ocean, feeding at the bottom in solid numbers. Most fish caught on hook and line are 20 to 40 pounds (9 to 18 kilograms), but older specimens are also hooked with some regularity.

> 1/4 cup (60 mL) butter, plus more for brushing
> 1/4 cup (60 mL) diced celery
> 1/4 cup (60 mL) chopped onion
> 1/2 tsp (2 mL) salt
> 1/2 tsp (2 mL) thyme
> 1/2 tsp (2 mL) savory
> 2 cups (500 mL) breadcrumbs or cornmeal
> 1 tomato, chopped
>
> 2 × 1 lb (454 g) halibut steaks

Preheat oven to 450°F (230°C). Grease baking dish. Melt butter in medium skillet. Add celery and onion and cook until soft. Add salt, thyme and savory. Stir in breadcrumbs and toss lightly. Add tomato.

Sandwich stuffing between halibut steaks. Brush with melted butter and place in shallow baking dish. Bake for about 30 minutes until fish flakes easily with a fork. Serve hot.

Try with This  **Skillet Potatoes**

Serves 6 to 8

2 to 3 lbs (900 g to 1.4 kg) small potatoes, unpeeled
water
2 Tbsp (30 mL) canola oil
1 Tbsp (15 mL) chopped fresh parsley
salt and pepper, to taste

Place potatoes in cast-iron pan with just enough water to cover. Place pan on burner, grill or open fire. Once water has boiled away (about 30 minutes), check tenderness of potatoes. If potatoes have not reached desired tenderness, continue to cook in pan until skins are crispy. Drizzle with oil and parsley and sprinkle with salt and pepper.

Halibut Skewers with Tarragon

Serves 4

Halibut are the largest member of the flatfish family, with distinctive dark grey to black on the top and whitish on the underside. At birth, halibut have an eye on each side of their head in the typical configuration found in cod or mackerel. By the time they reach six to eight months of age, however, one eye begins to move to the other side, giving them a more flatfish appearance. That eye later darkens to match the grey-black colour of the fish's topside. The black-on-white colour combination of the halibut is no fluke either. The dark surface colour allows the halibut to blend in with the sunlight shining through the water, whereas the light underside matches perfectly with the ocean floor.

1/3 cup (75 mL) olive oil
1/4 cup (60 mL) white-wine vinegar
2 Tbsp (30 mL) minced shallots
1 Tbsp (15 mL) chopped fresh tarragon
1 Tbsp (15 mL) Dijon mustard
salt and pepper, to taste

1 lb (454 g) halibut fillets, cut into 1-inch (2.5 cm) chunks

6 cups (1.5 L) mixed baby greens

Preheat grill or barbecue to medium-high. Mix oil, vinegar, shallots, tarragon and mustard in small bowl and whisk to blend. Season with salt and pepper and set aside.

Place fish in glass dish and pour half of tarragon mixture over fish. Turn to coat, and marinate for about 15 minutes at room temperature. Thread fish onto 4 metal skewers, about 5 chunks per skewer.

Place skewers on grill and cook for about 5 minutes, turning occasionally, until fish is just opaque in centre.

Meanwhile, toss baby greens with remaining tarragon mixture. Divide salad among 4 plates. Place fish skewers atop greens and serve immediately.

Sautéed Halibut Steaks

Serves 4

Pacific halibut are North America's king of the flatfish and can grow to enormous sizes. Halibut in excess of 100 pounds (45 kilograms) are landed by sport fishermen each year. On June 11, 1996, the halibut fishing world was rocked with the news of Jack Tragis's giant catch. While fishing out of Alaska's famous Dutch Harbor—the setting for the Discovery Channel's popular television show *The Deadliest Catch*—Tragis pulled in a truly monstrous halibut weighing an unbelievable 459 pounds (208.2 kilograms). The Tragis halibut stands as the largest-ever caught by a recreational angler.

4 × 11 to 14 oz (310 to 400 g) halibut steaks
salt and pepper, to taste
1 1/2 cups (375 mL) whole-wheat flour
2 Tbsp (30 mL) butter
1 Tbsp (15 mL) canola oil

1 green pepper, thinly sliced
1 celery rib, thinly sliced
1 cup (250 mL) fish stock, heated (*see* Tip, p. 97)
1/2 tsp (2 mL) cornstarch
2 Tbsp (30 mL) cold water

Preheat oven to 400°F (205°C) and grease baking pan. Season halibut steaks with salt and pepper and dredge in flour. Heat butter and oil in large skillet over medium-high. Add halibut steaks and cook for about 10 minutes, turning once.

Transfer halibut steaks to prepared pan. Drizzle with remaining oil and butter from skillet. Bake for 5 to 7 minutes. Remove fish to serving platter and place in warming oven.

Add green pepper and celery to skillet and season with salt and pepper. Cook over medium for 5 minutes, then add stock, cornstarch and water. Simmer until mixture thickens slightly.

Transfer vegetables to serving platter and serve immediately.

Savoury Halibut Enchiladas

Serves 8

Halibut charter boat operators like Terry Weaver know a few things about catching trophy-size Pacific halibut. Skipper Terry has an intimate knowledge of halibut fishing gained from over 25 years of commercial and sport fishing in the waters around Prince Rupert and the north coast of British Columbia. Halibut gurus like Weaver are confident about the fish they catch and always put their client's safety first: Weaver possesses a master's certificate in Marine Safety. "Although we routinely limit out," says Weaver, "our customer policy remains 'No Fish, No Pay.'" According to Weaver, the biggest halibut caught recently in Chatham Sound near Prince Rupert was 324 pounds (147 kilograms), and fish over 100 pounds (45 kilograms) are a very real possibility. Now that's a lot of delicious meals!

> 2 lbs (900 g) halibut fillets, cut into large pieces
> 1/4 tsp (1 mL) garlic powder
> salt and pepper, to taste
> 1 bunch green onions, chopped
> 1 green pepper, finely chopped
> 1/2 cup (125 mL) sour cream
> 1/4 cup (60 mL) mayonnaise
> 2 cups (500 mL) shredded Cheddar cheese, *divided*
>
> 2 × 10 oz (284 mL) cans enchilada sauce, *divided*
> 8 tortilla shells
> 2 avocados, peeled, pitted and sliced

Preheat oven to 375°F (190°C). Season halibut with garlic powder, salt and pepper. Place green onions, green pepper, sour cream, mayonnaise and 1 cup (250 mL) cheese in bowl; stir to combine. Add fish pieces and gently stir them in.

Pour 1/2 can of enchilada sauce into large non-stick baking dish. Pour 1 can of enchilada sauce into bowl. Dip each tortilla shell into sauce in bowl, shaking off excess. Divide mayo mixture among tortillas, placing it down centre of each tortilla. Roll up tortillas shells and place in baking dish with seams tucked under. Pour remaining sauce over top and sprinkle with 1 cup (250 mL) cheese. Bake, covered, for 40 to 45 minutes. Top with avocado slices and serve hot.

Mackerel with Cream Sauce

Serves 4

The Atlantic mackerel is a fixture in waters of the eastern provinces. According to my mackerel expert pal Grant Bailey, when targeting this torpedo-shaped quarry, a leader rigged with two to four "mackerel flies" above the metal lure is recommended. Any spoon will work, with Red Devils and Crippled Minnows being perhaps the most common. Once hooked, these speedy fish supply fast escape tactics, which is what they are built for, after all. Mackerel provide great sport on a light spinning-rod, especially when multiple fish have teamed up on you.

1/4 cup (60 mL) chopped mushrooms
1 tomato, chopped
1/4 cup (60 mL) breadcrumbs or cornmeal
4 Tbsp (60 mL) butter, *divided*
1/4 tsp (1 mL) lemon juice
4 medium mackerel, backbones removed (*see* Tip, p. 103)

2 Tbsp (30 mL) flour
1 cup (250 mL) cold milk
salt and pepper, to taste

Preheat oven to 400°F (205°C). In bowl, mix mushrooms, tomato, breadcrumbs, 2 Tbsp (30 mL) butter and lemon juice. Stuff mackerel with mixture and place in non-stick baking pan, cover with foil and bake for 15 minutes.

For sauce, heat 2 Tbsp (30 mL) butter and flour in saucepan and cook for 3 to 4 minutes. Lower heat and slowly add milk. Bring to a boil, then lower heat and stir until slightly reduced. Whisk in salt and pepper. Pour sauce over fish and serve.

Roasted Mackerel with Dijon Mustard

Serves 4

According to the New Brunswick Fish Factsheet, mackerel have no swim bladder (often called an air bladder) and therefore must swim continuously to avoid sinking. The lack of swim bladder also allows mackerel to change depth rapidly. On their long annual migrations, mackerel often travel in very dense schools, especially in the spring and fall. These schools tend to be composed of identical-sized fish swimming together in unison, much like a team of synchronized swimmers. As with halibut, the mackerel's body is counter-shaded, with a darker colour on top and lighter colour below. The top half of the body exhibits the characteristic 23 to 33 dark wavy bands, and the bottom half shines with a steel blue or copper iridescence. They are magnificent-looking fish.

> 4 × 5 to 6 oz (140 to 170 g) mackerel fillets, with skin
> 1 tsp (5 mL) salt
> 1/8 tsp (0.5 mL) pepper
> 2 Tbsp (30 mL) olive oil
> 3 Tbsp (45 mL) Dijon mustard

Preheat broiler. Cut shallow diagonal slashes into mackerel 1 inch (2.5 cm) apart. Season fillets with salt and pepper. Coat mackerel with oil and cover completely with Dijon mustard. Place on shallow baking sheet and broil mackerel until skin is brown and crispy.

Try with This  **Old-fashioned Onion Rings**

Serves 4

canola or peanut oil, for deep-frying
2 large onions, cut into 1/4-inch (6 mm) slices
1 1/4 cups (300 mL) flour
1 tsp (5 mL) baking powder
1 tsp (5 mL) salt
3/4 cup (175 mL) breadcrumbs
1 egg
1 cup (250 mL) milk
seasoning salt, to taste

Place oil in deep-fryer and heat to 365°F (185°C). Using your hands, separate onion slices into rings and set aside.

In bowl, combine flour, baking powder and salt. Coat onion rings with flour mixture until completely coated, and then set rings aside on parchment paper–covered baking sheet. Spread breadcrumbs on plate and set aside.

Add egg and milk to flour mixture and stir to combine. Dip floured rings into batter to fully coat and allow excess batter to drip off. One at a time, place rings in breadcrumbs and allow to coat. Return rings to parchment-covered baking sheet.

Deep-fry rings a few at a time for 2 to 3 minutes until golden brown, making sure oil returns to 365°F (185°C) before adding each new batch. Remove to paper towels to drain. Sprinkle with seasoning salt. Serve immediately.

Simple Mustard Mackerel on the Grill

Serves 4

In the Shediac area of New Brunswick, sport fishing for mackerel is taken quite seriously. When the mackerel schools are running, copious fish can be found around piers and bridges, where they corral the bait fish to create a feeding frenzy. And you can't miss the mackerel run either—you will notice anglers standing and casting side by side, reeling in these silver torpedoes hand over fist. According to the Department of Fisheries and Oceans, no fishing licence is required to fish these tidal waters. There are several techniques for catching mackerel consistently but the use of jigging spoons seems to be one of the most effective. These fish respond to flash and movement, so any small, heavy spoon casted and jigged back to shore generally works. And if you happen to be skunked while out fishing, do not despair: the town of Shediac boasts a number of great fish and seafood restaurants.

> 4 × 6 oz (170 g) mackerel fillets, with skin
> 1/4 tsp (1 mL) salt
> 1/4 tsp (1 mL) pepper
> 2 Tbsp (30 mL) prepared yellow mustard

Preheat grill or barbecue to medium. Season mackerel fillets with salt and pepper. Coat each fish with mustard and grill for 10 to 15 minutes on each side, turning often. Serve immediately.

Spicy Grilled Mackerel

Serves 4

According to the Department of Fisheries and Oceans, there are several commercial fishing techniques for harvesting mackerel. In Nova Scotia, gillnet and trap net fishing for mackerel takes place primarily in June and July, as does gillnet fishery in the Gulf of St. Lawrence. Most nets are fixed in place, except for a drift fishery in Chaleur Bay and in the part of the Gulf between New Brunswick, Prince Edward Island and the Magdalen Islands. In late summer and fall, commercial mackerel fishermen also carry out hand line fishery in the Gulf of St. Lawrence and Nova Scotia. A specialized net called a purse seine is used on the west and east coasts of Newfoundland and in Cape Breton. According to government statistics, mackerel numbers are in no apparent danger.

1 Tbsp (15 mL) coriander seeds
1 Tbsp (15 mL) black mustard seeds
1 Tbsp (15 mL) cumin seeds
1 tsp (5 mL) black peppercorns
1 dried hot chili pepper, chopped

8 × 4 oz (115 g) mackerel fillets
1 cup (250 mL) Dijon mustard

Heat dry frying pan over medium and add coriander seeds, mustard seeds, cumin seeds and peppercorns and toast for 2 to 3 minutes, shaking from time to time until mustard seeds are popping and spices are aromatic. Blend toasted spices with chili pepper into smooth powder in coffee grinder or with pestle and mortar. Set aside.

Preheat barbecue or grill to high. Cover both sides of mackerel fillets with spice mixture. Place fillets on grill and cook for 5 minutes, turning often. When cooked, mackerel should be slightly dark brown to black, and no longer soft to the touch. Serve with Dijon mustard on side.

Baked Muskellunge

Serves 4

The muskellunge, or "muskie" as it is most often called in Canada, is considered one of the most difficult game fish to catch. The muskie comes by its nickname "the fish of 10,000 casts" honestly, because most anglers will never catch or even see a muskie in their lifetimes. They only feed when absolutely necessary, and on very large prey. "Lunge" have been known to snap up ducks, muskrats, turtles and other game fish such as walleye and northern pike. Female muskies weighing between 30 and 40 pounds (13.5 to 18 kilograms) are caught each year across Canada. Most of these trophy-size fish are live-released to ensure the sustainability of the species.

> 4 muskellunge steaks (*see* Tip, p. 74)
> salt and pepper, to taste
> 3 Tbsp (45 mL) butter
> 3 Tbsp (45 mL) minced onion
> 1/4 tsp (1 mL) dried thyme
>
> 1 1/2 cups (375 mL) milk
> 1 Tbsp (15 mL) flour
> 1 × 10 oz (284 mL) can condensed cream of chicken soup
> 1 Tbsp (15 mL) horseradish

Season each muskie steak with salt and pepper. In cast-iron skillet, heat butter over medium and sauté steaks for 10 minutes, turning once. Add onion and thyme and continue cooking until fish flakes easily with a fork. Set aside in warming oven.

In saucepan, blend milk, flour, soup and horseradish. Bring sauce to a slow boil over medium, stirring until smooth. Pour sauce over muskie steaks and serve immediately.

Muskie with Egg Noodles

Serves 4

Although I hate to admit it, being the avid muskellunge conservationist that I am, one of my most memorable fish meals was the dish I prepared at our Témiscaminge moose camp in 1994. It was the first muskie I ever caught, so I decided to honour the fish by saving it for a very important meal. There was just something about the texture and flavour of that muskie that I never forgot. I have practised catch and release since that first muskie because they are a very fragile fish, but I don't believe it is wrong to keep the occasional smaller fish for consumption, regardless of the species.

> 1 × 16 oz (454 g) package egg noodles
> 1 × 8 oz (227 mL) can pasta sauce
> 1 lb (454 g) boneless muskellunge fillets
> 3 cups (750 mL) shredded mozzarella cheese

Preheat oven to 375°F (190°C). Cook egg noodles according to package directions. Spray large oven-proof dish with non-stick cooking spray and fill 3/4 full with noodles. Spoon 1/4 pasta sauce over egg noodles. Place layer of fillets on top of noodles. Add more sauce over fillets to cover. Cover dish with foil and bake for 15 minutes. Remove cover and sprinkle mozzarella cheese over top. Return to oven and bake, uncovered, for 5 minutes. Fillets are done when they flake easily with a fork and cheese is slightly browned.

Try with This

Spinach Salad

Serves 8

1 lb (454 g) spinach, rinsed well and torn into bite-sized pieces
1 cup (250 mL) dried cranberries
2 Tbsp (30 mL) toasted sesame seeds
1/2 cup (125 mL) white sugar
2 tsp (10 mL) minced onion
1/4 cup (60 mL) white wine vinegar
1/2 cup (125 mL) olive oil

Place spinach into large salad bowl and set aside. In medium bowl, whisk together remaining ingredients. Slowly add to spinach; toss and serve.

Blackened Perch Fillets

Serves 4

Don't let their meagre size fool you: coldwater perch are some of the sweetest, best-tasting fish you will find anywhere. In regions of Canada with an active winter ice-fishing season and solid number of fish, such as Ontario's Lake Simcoe, perch are targeted with regularity. Although perch can be somewhat labour-intensive to clean and prepare, you will be greatly rewarded once they hit the table. Perch meat is firm-textured, low in fat and explodes with flavour when it hits the palate.

> 2 Tbsp (30 mL) paprika
> 1 tsp (5 mL) garlic powder
> 1/2 tsp (2 mL) cayenne pepper
> 1/2 tsp (2 mL) pepper
> 1/2 tsp (2 mL) thyme
> 1/2 tsp (2 mL) oregano
>
> 1 lb (454 g) perch (8 to 10 fillets)
> 2 Tbsp (30 mL) melted butter

Coat cast-iron skillet with non-stick cooking spray and preheat over high. Mix paprika, garlic powder, cayenne pepper, pepper, thyme and oregano in small bowl. Coat fillets completely in mixture. Place fish in hot skillet and pour melted butter on top. Cook each side until almost charred, then flip over and cook other side. Serve piping hot!

Try with This  **Fish Sauce with a Bite**

Makes 2 cups (500 mL)

1 1/2 cups (375 mL) butter
1 tsp (5 mL) prepared yellow mustard
2 Tbsp (30 mL) chili sauce
2 Tbsp (30 mL) lemon juice
salt and pepper, to taste (optional)

In medium saucepan over medium, stir butter and mustard until smooth. Add chili sauce and lemon juice. Continue to stir until smooth. Cover and simmer 3 minutes until thickened. Taste and adjust seasoning with salt and pepper if desired.

Perch Casserole

Serves 4

Although yellow perch are a more plentiful relative of the walleye, they are rarely used in wild fish recipes. I can't understand why after I discovered how tasty they really are. They are susceptible to yellow grub, black spot disease and gill anchor worm, but none of these parasites are of any real concern when it comes to filleting or preparing perch for the table. The meat is opaque and clean and cooks up into a brilliant shade of white, flaking easily when touched with a fork. Perch truly are one of Canada's great untapped resources.

> 2 lbs (900 g) perch (16 to 20 fillets)
> 10 small potatoes, peeled and quartered
> 2 × 10 oz (284 mL) cans condensed cream of celery soup
> 2 1/2 cups (625 mL) milk
> 1/4 cup (60 mL) diced onion
> 1/2 cup (125 mL) diced ham
> 1/4 cup (60 mL) grated mozzarella cheese

Preheat oven to 250°F (120°C). Coat medium baking dish with non-stick cooking spray. Place fillets in dish. Arrange potatoes around outside. Heat soup, milk, onion and ham in saucepan and stir, and then pour evenly in dish. Sprinkle with cheese and bake for 2 hours.

Try with This 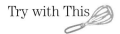 ## Green Bean Salad

Serves 4

2 Tbsp (30 mL) chopped fresh oregano
2 Tbsp (30 mL) olive oil
2 Tbsp (30 mL) white-wine vinegar
2 tsp (10 mL) Dijon mustard
1/2 tsp (2 mL) salt
1/2 tsp (2 mL) pepper
14 oz (396 g) fresh or frozen green beans,
    slightly blanched until crisp-tender

In bowl, whisk together all ingredients except beans. Add beans and toss. Cover and refrigerate for 1 hour before serving.

Catfish Tacos (p. 32)

Northern Pike Chili (p. 77)

Baked Perch with Cheese Sauce

Serves 4

Yellow perch spawn during the springtime when the water temperature is between 7 and 12°C. The female perch deposits 5000 to 40,000 eggs during the spawn. Perch would never win any parent-of-the-year awards: not only do they abandon their offspring, they often resort to eating them if necessary. Perch enjoy most cool-water, nutrient-rich lakes but may also live in large, slowly moving rivers. They are often seen travelling in schools in search of food with their fins stretched outward—their small set of spiny fins are their only real defence against other predatory fish.

> 1 1/2 lbs (680 g) perch (12 to 15 fillets)
> 3 Tbsp (45 mL) butter
> 3 Tbsp (45 mL) flour
> 1 tsp (5 mL) salt
> 1/2 tsp (2 mL) dry mustard
> 1/4 tsp (1 mL) dried dill
> 1 1/2 cups (375 mL) half-and-half cream
> 4 oz (115 g) small salad shrimp
> 1 1/2 cups (375 mL) grated Cheddar cheese, *divided*

Preheat oven to 350°F (175°C). Arrange perch fillets in greased baking dish. In saucepan, melt butter, then mix in flour. Bring to a slight boil, stirring. Add salt, mustard and dill. Remove from heat and slowly add cream. Place back on heat, add shrimp and 1 cup (250 mL) cheese and mix until thickened. Slowly pour over fish and sprinkle 1/2 cup (125 mL) cheese on top. Bake for about 30 minutes.

Perch Fry

Serves 6

Although the most common size for the spunky yellow perch is 6 to 8 inches (15 to 20 centimetres), they do grow bigger than that in certain areas. Trophy or jumbo perch, as they are often called, have garnered the attention of anglers across the country. Although the largest-ever perch was caught in the Delaware River back in 1865 and weighed over 4 pounds (1.8 kilograms), it would be rare to see one in Canada measuring much more than 12 inches (30 centimetres) and tipping the scales at even 1 pound (454 grams) or so. Anglers in Ontario's Lake Simcoe—regarded as perhaps the most productive yellow perch fishery in the world—continue to buck the trend by catching jumbos in excess of 12 inches (30 centimetres) each year!

1 cup (250 mL) flour
2 whole eggs, beaten
1 1/2 cups (375 mL) sesame seeds
2 1/2 lbs (1.1 kg) perch fillets
salt and pepper, to taste

1 Tbsp (15 mL) butter
1 Tbsp (15 mL) vegetable oil

In 3 separate bowls, place flour, eggs and sesame seeds. Sprinkle perch fillets with salt and pepper on both sides. Dip each fillet in flour, shaking off excess, then into beaten eggs and then into sesame seeds, coating completely.

Heat butter and oil in large skillet over medium. Fry fillets for about 8 minutes, turning once, until crispy on outside and opaque on inside. Drain on paper towels and serve.

Baked Lemon Perch

Serves 4

Not only are yellow perch one of the most prevalent freshwater fish species in Canada, they make a nutritious and tasty meal. Perch are also listed as having one of the lowest concentrations of mercury, which means one can enjoy and experiment with the great perch recipes in this book without fear of reprisal.

Baked Lemon Perch, continued

1 tsp (5 mL) grated lemon peel
1/3 cup (75 mL) lemon juice
1/4 cup (60 mL) canola oil
1/4 tsp (60 mL) salt
1/4 tsp (60 mL) pepper
1 Tbsp (15 mL) chopped parsley
12 perch fillets (6 perch), boneless
1 lemon, cut into wedges

Preheat oven to 375°F (190°C) and grease medium baking dish. In bowl, combine lemon peel, lemon juice, oil, salt, pepper and parsley. Mix well. Add perch fillets to bowl and stir, making sure to cover each fillet with mixture. Transfer to prepared baking dish. Bake for 15 minutes until perch are slightly brown and meat flakes easily with a fork. Garnish with lemon wedges.

Try with This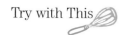

Dill Sauce

Makes 4 cups (1 L)

2 Tbsp (30 mL) shortening
2 Tbsp (30 mL) butter
1 cup (250 mL) chopped, firmly packed fresh dill
salt, to taste
2 cups (500 mL) chicken broth
2 to 3 Tbsp (30 to 45 mL) flour
1 cup (250 mL) milk
1/2 cup (125 mL) half-and-half cream, *divided*
1/4 cup (60 mL) vinegar
juice from 1/2 lemon
1/4 tsp (1 mL) white pepper
1 cup (250 mL) sour cream

In large saucepan over medium, melt shortening and butter. Add dill and salt and stir until completely heated. Add chicken broth and bring to a boil. In small bowl, mix flour, milk and 1/4 cup (60 mL) cream. Whisk mixture into boiling liquid and reduce heat. Add vinegar, lemon juice and pepper and simmer for 20 minutes, stirring occasionally. In small bowl, mix remaining 1/4 cup (60 mL) cream with sour cream. Slowly spoon some sauce into cream mixture to warm the mixture. Add remaining sauce, cover and keep warm until ready to serve.

Cheesy Pike

Serves 4

Northern pike are perhaps the most underrated freshwater fish when it comes to table fare. Possibly it is their unsavoury predatory behaviour or pungent live smell that has given them a bad name. Provided they are filleted properly and carefully skinned so that the protective slime layer does not come in contact with the flesh, pike meat is white, flaky and bursting with taste. By the same token, northern pikes must never be cooked or barbecued with the skin on, because it gives the meat an unpleasant muddy taste. When prepared properly, though, the northern pike is one of the most pleasant-tasting fish around—one of my personal favourites.

> 1 lb (454 g) northern pike fillets, cut into 4 equal servings
> 1 egg
> 2 Tbsp (30 mL) milk
> 1/4 cup (60 mL) grated Parmesan cheese
> 1/4 cup (60 mL) breadcrumbs
> 1/2 tsp (2 mL) paprika
> 1/8 tsp (0.5 mL) pepper

Preheat oven to 475°F (245°C) and grease baking pan or sheet. Rinse fish under cold water and pat dry with paper towel. Blend egg and milk together on one plate and on another plate combine Parmesan cheese, breadcrumbs, paprika and pepper. First dip each fish piece in egg mixture, then roll in crumb mixture. Place coated fish in prepared pan and bake for 12 to 15 minutes until golden brown. Serve immediately.

 tip **SKINNING PIKE OR MUSKELLUNGE**

Members of the Esox family (pike and muskellunge) have a protective slime layer that can give the fish an unpleasant muddy taste, so it must be removed before cooking with a sharp fillet knife. For a whole fish, start at the tail and insert the tip of your knife along the inside edge of the skin, and carefully slice toward the head. For fish steaks, stand them up and cut through the skin at the backbone with a pair of scissors, then skin down each side of the steak to the bottom. Once the skin is removed, discard immediately and wash the fish in cool water. Try to keep the outside portion of the skin from ever touching the meat.

White Wine Braised Pike

Serves 8

Always be cautious when preparing northern pike: avoid the belly meat at all costs, since toxins such as mercury and other heavy metals tend to concentrate in this part of the fish. The same holds true when filleting other fish as well, especially larger, older specimens that have spent more time in the lake or river. Many anglers clean pike using what is called the 5-fillet method: a strip of meat is used off the back, two strips along the "Y" bones and two strips in front of the caudal fin or tail. It is a technique I have used for years with considerable success. When prepared and cooked properly, northern pike's distinct, bold taste will rival that of many other more popular wild Canadian fish.

1 1/2 cups (375 mL) water
1 onion, sliced
1 carrot, sliced
1 celery rib with leaves, chopped

4 shallots, diced
3 tomatoes, diced, or 3 canned tomatoes, squashed
5 to 6 lbs (2.3 to 2.7 kg) northern pike, cleaned (*see* p. 5) but not filleted (*see* Tip, p. 74)
1/2 cup (125 mL) dry white wine

salt and pepper, to taste

Preheat oven to 400°F (205°C). Boil water in medium saucepan, then add onion, carrot and celery. Simmer until reduced to 1/2 cup (125 mL) of liquid. Strain and set liquid aside. Spread shallots and tomatoes in medium non-stick baking or casserole dish. Lay pike in dish and then pour in white wine and 1/2 of retained liquid.

Bake fish for 30 minutes, basting often. When fish is done, transfer to serving platter. Strain remaining liquid into bowl (discard solids), add salt and pepper and then pour over fish. Serve immediately.

Grilled Northern Pike
with Pine Nuts

Serves 4

A wild fish shore lunch, whether with northern pike or some other fish, is a tradition everyone should enjoy once in their lives. The idea of the traditional shore lunch is that whatever species you happen to catch is cooked up fresh for lunch along the lake or river shoreline. In order to make your shore lunch a success, you will need to have a few pieces of important equipment: two large skillets, fresh cooking oil, butter, spices, utensils, flour or fish crisp, an easy side dish like rice or potatoes and a heat source. You may use a Coleman stove, but the more traditional shore lunch is carried out over an open fire. After enjoying freshly caught fish cooked in the great outdoors, you will never want to eat at home again.

> 1 tsp (5 mL) vegetable oil
> 6 Tbsp (90 mL) pine nuts
> 2 Tbsp (30 mL) butter
> 6 shallots or small scallions, trimmed and sliced diagonally
> 2 lbs (900 g) northern pike fillets
>
> 1 to 2 lemon wedges
> salt and pepper, to taste

Heat oil in medium skillet. Add pine nuts and stir until golden brown. Set pine nuts aside on paper towel. Melt butter in same skillet. Add shallots and sauté for 2 minutes. Stir in pine nuts and then remove from heat.

On medium non-stick grill, cook fish for 5 to 7 minutes per side (based on the 10 minutes per inch rule—fillets are measured at their thickest point). Squeeze fresh lemon juice over fish and season with salt and pepper. Serve immediately.

Northern Pike Chili

(*see* photo p. 70)

Serves 4

Northern pike are one of Canada's largest freshwater fish. They can strike fear in the hearts of any members of their aquatic environment, no matter whether small or adult. Although large in size, pike are not known to be big fighters in the water. As my father always said, "With pike, half the fight is in the water and the other half is in the boat." One time, while fishing in northern Québec, I landed a 10-pound (4.5-kilogram) pike in 5 minutes with relative ease, only to battle with the thrashing fish for another 10 minutes in the boat. Pike go crazy when they are off the hook and can cause serious injury. We released that fish a short time later and it swam off as if nothing had happened...but of course, not before knocking over two tackle boxes and bending the landing net in half.

1 Tbsp (15 mL) olive oil
1/2 cup (125 mL) diced red pepper
2 garlic cloves, minced
1/2 cup (125 mL) chopped onion

2 × 14 oz (398 mL) cans crushed tomatoes
1 × 14 oz (398 mL) can kidney beans, drained
2 Tbsp (30 mL) cornstarch
1/4 cup (60 mL) water
2 Tbsp (30 mL) parsley
1 tsp (5 mL) chili powder, or to taste
1/8 tsp (0.5 mL) cayenne pepper

1 lb (454 g) northern pike fillets, cut into 1-inch (2.5 cm) cubes

Heat olive oil in saucepan and add red pepper, garlic and onion. Sauté until slightly brown. Add all remaining ingredients except pike. Cover and simmer until mixture begins to thicken. Stir occasionally to keep from sticking.

Add fish and simmer for 10 minutes until fish is fully cooked. Serve with steamed rice and fresh bread.

Pike with Orange Rice Stuffing

Serves 4 to 5

During a fishing trip to Québec's famous Lake Mistassini in 1979, I put four fish species to the ultimate taste test. Mistassini is the province's largest body of water; it also boasts world-class angling for northern pike, walleye, lake trout and whitefish. One night, we decided to create a head-to-head "table challenge" to see which species was the best. We had a very simple meal consisting of fillets from each type of fish, slowly pan-seared in butter with seasoning and covered to get a steamed effect. Once the fish were fully cooked, my father Rathwell, our friend David Batty, his son Steve and I dug into our fish cornucopia. After all was said and done, we all agreed the northern pike was the best of the bunch! The moral of the story is, don't discount pike the next time you serve fish.

3 to 4 lbs (1.4 to 1.8 kg) pike, cleaned (*see* p. 5) but not filleted (*see* Tip, p. 74)

1/4 cup (60 mL) butter
1 cup (250 mL) chopped celery with leaves
3 Tbsp (45 mL) chopped onion
2 Tbsp (30 mL) grated orange rind

3/4 cup (175 mL) water
1/2 cup (125 mL) orange juice
2 Tbsp (30 mL) lemon juice
1/2 tsp (2 mL) salt

1 cup (250 mL) precooked rice

Preheat oven to 400°F (205°C). Remove scales, fins, head and tail from pike (*see* Tip, p. 99). Set aside. Grease baking pan and set aside.

Melt butter in saucepan over medium and stir in celery, onion and orange rind. Cook until soft. Mix in water, orange juice, lemon juice and salt. Bring to a boil and stir in rice. Cover, remove from heat and let stand for 5 minutes.

Stuff fish with orange rice, then place on prepared pan and brush with melted butter. Bake for 30 minutes until fish is opaque and separates easily from bone. Serve immediately.

Northern Québec Pike Fry

(see photo p. 87)

Serves 4

When it comes to fishing, every avid angler can recall in vivid detail the story of the big one that got away. For me, one time was in the early 1990s while fishing in Beaven Lake with my pal Diederic Godin. We had just made a trolling pass along Priest Point when suddenly my fishing rod buckled in the rod holder. "Fish on!" I yelled. As I reached for the rod to set the hook, I could not believe the weight of the fish. "It's got to be a muskie!" I yelled to Diederic, and then a minute later Diederic's rod took off also. "A double header!" we screamed in unison, although we quickly found out we had both hooked the same fish. Suddenly my line went limp and Diederic was on his own, with the fish now nearing the boat. It was then we noticed two important details. This bruiser was no muskie: it was the largest northern pike we had ever seen, easily weighing 25 to 30 pounds (11 to 13 kilograms). The second thing we noticed was the monster pike was no longer hooked to anything, and merely had Diederic's line wrapped around its gills. Before we could get the net on her, she was gone. We both stared at each other, dumbfounded, and though it was nearly 20 years ago, I remember it to this day.

3 lbs (1.4 kg) boneless pike fillets

3 cups (750 mL) milk
2 eggs, beaten
1/2 tsp (2 mL) garlic powder
1/2 tsp (2 mL) onion salt
1/2 tsp (2 mL) salt
1/2 tsp (2 mL) pepper
2 cups (500 mL) breadcrumbs or cornmeal

3 cups (750 mL) vegetable oil
1 lemon, cut into wedges

Remove any bones from fillets. Trim off dark edges or belly meat. Pat fish dry with paper towel and set aside.

In medium mixing bowl, combine milk, eggs, garlic powder, onion salt, salt and pepper. Mix well. Place breadcrumbs in separate bowl.

Heat oil in large, steep-sided skillet on medium-high. Dip each fillet into milk and egg mixture, allowing excess mixture to run off, then dredge fillet in breadcrumbs. Place each coated fillet in hot oil and fry for about 15 minutes, turning once, until golden brown. Transfer to serving dish, garnish with lemon wedges and serve.

Canadian Maple Salmon

Serves 4

What better way to enjoy two distinct Canadian favourites—salmon and real Canadian maple syrup—than together in one symbiotic dish? As with other meats traditionally served with real maple syrup, your salmon will spring to life in this sinfully sweet concoction. It is one dish where substituting imitation syrup for the real thing is simply not an option. The enticing flavour and aroma of natural maple syrup forms a beautiful marriage with the freshly cooked salmon. Did you know that maple syrup quality is gauged by colour, with light gold-coloured syrup being of milder flavour and superior grade than the lower-grade dark amber syrup?

> 1/4 cup (60 mL) pure Canadian maple syrup
> 1 tsp (5 mL) Dijon mustard
> 2 Tbsp (30 mL) soy sauce
> 1 Tbsp (15 mL) lemon juice
>
> 1 1/4 lbs (560 g) salmon fillets
> 2 Tbsp (30 mL) sliced shallots

Place all ingredients except salmon and shallots in shallow dish; stir to combine. Remove and reserve 1/4 cup (60 mL) marinade; set aside. Lay salmon fillets in dish, then use spoon to scoop some marinade over top. Refrigerate for about 30 minutes.

Preheat oven to 400°F (205°C). Remove fish from marinade; set aside marinade. Place fillets in baking dish and bake for 15 to 20 minutes, smearing with marinade occasionally, until fish flakes easily.

Drizzle reserved marinade over salmon, top with shallots and serve.

Wild Salmon en Papillote

Serves 4

Salmon makes an ideal meal choice for nutrition and health reasons because they were recently discovered to have some of the highest levels of omega-3 fatty acids—an enzyme that helps reduce the risk of cardiovascular anomalies. Although salmon are considered one of the world's healthiest foods, keep in mind that smoking salmon has been found to substantially reduce its omega-3 content. Wild salmon contain only 3000 milligrams of omega-3s for a 6-ounce (170 gram) serving, compared with farmed salmon with 4500 milligrams. It has been noted, however, that farmed salmon may exhibit higher levels of toxic PCBs.

> **4 × 4 to 6 oz (115 to 170 g) wild salmon fillets**
> **4 leeks, white part only, thinly sliced**
> **1 bunch dill, finely chopped**
> **1/4 cup (60 mL) white wine**
> **salt and pepper, to taste**
> **1/4 cup (60 mL) unsalted butter, _divided_ into 4 pieces**
>
> **1 lemon, sliced**

Preheat oven to 350°F (175°C). Take 4 × 20-inch (50 cm) sheets of foil or parchment paper and fold them in half, then cut heart shapes a few inches larger than fillets and lay out flat on work surface. Arrange 1 fillet on each heart shape near centre; place 1/4 of leeks and dill on each fillet. Sprinkle fillets with wine, salt and pepper and top with piece of butter.

Fold foil or paper in half and make small overlapping folds around heart shapes to seal fish in securely. Place packets on baking sheet and bake for about 15 minutes. Packets will be puffed and brownish; use caution when transferring to serving plates and when opening because they will emit gusts of steam. Serve garnished with lemon slices.

Salmon Carpaccio

Serves 4

Of the five species of Pacific salmon, the pink salmon are the shortest and by far the smallest. The average pink typically weighs between 4 and 6 pounds (1.8 and 2.7 kilograms). Even though pinks rarely exceed 10 pounds (4.5 kilograms), they are still one sport fish to be reckoned with. During fall migration, male pink salmon undergo several morphological changes, including the development of a large lower jaw known as a kipe, as well as a prominently humped back. For this reason, pinks are often referred to as humpbacks.

1 1/2 lbs (680 g) salmon fillets
1/2 cup (125 mL) finely chopped basil
1/2 cup (125 mL) finely chopped Italian parsley
1/2 cup (125 mL) finely chopped thyme
2 Tbsp (30 mL) crushed black peppercorns

1/2 cup (125 mL) red wine
1 cup (250 mL) olive oil, *divided*
1 bunch green onions, washed

1 lb (454 g) asparagus, washed
1 Tbsp (15 mL) chopped shallots
2 garlic cloves, finely chopped
1/4 cup (60 mL) dry white wine
1/4 cup (60 mL) water
1 large bay leaf

2 to 3 Tbsp (30 to 45 mL) vegetable oil
fresh parsley or basil, for garnish

Slice salmon into 6-inch (15 cm) strips. Spread herbs on baking sheet. Rub peppercorns into salmon, then roll in herbs and refrigerate for 2 to 3 hours.

Heat red wine to a slow simmer in small saucepan and reduce by 3/4. Let cool slightly. In blender, mix reduced red wine and 1/3 cup (75 mL) olive oil. Remove to bowl and set aside. Clean blender. Drop green onions briefly in boiling water and rinse with cold water. Pat dry and purée in blender. Add 1/3 cup (75 mL) olive oil slowly while blender is on. Set aside.

Snap tough ends off asparagus and peel stems. In large skillet, heat 1/3 cup (75 mL) olive oil. Sauté shallots and garlic. Add asparagus, white wine, water and bay leaf. Cover and cook for 4 to 6 minutes. Remove from stock; let cool but do not refrigerate. Discard stock.

Heat vegetable oil in cast-iron skillet over high until hot. Quickly sear salmon for about 30 seconds on each side. Cool immediately in refrigerator. Serve with asparagus spears. Drizzle with oils and garnish with fresh parsley or basil.

Chinese-style Salmon
Serves 4

Conservation and sport-fishing in Canada have always gone hand-in-hand. Each province and territory has a department in charge of managing our natural fish species and their respective fishing seasons. Sport fishing seasons are based on biological data with individual species' behaviour and life cycle taken into consideration. Angling is never permitted during spawning, and allowable catch numbers and possession limits are set based on fish numbers on each given body of water. Even though creel limits (i.e., catch limits) are there to control the number of fish kept for consumption, it is our duty as responsible Canadians to limit our catch where possible. As a nation, we have prided ourselves on keeping only what we need and trying not to overharvest. Fish are renewable natural resources to be enjoyed by future generations.

> 4 × 8 oz (225 g) salmon fillets
> 1/4 cup (60 mL) soy sauce
> 1 tsp (5 mL) finely ground ginger
> 1/3 cup (75 mL) sweet chili sauce
>
> 4 green onions, thinly sliced
> salt and pepper, to taste

Preheat oven to 300°F (150°C). Lay salmon fillets in non-stick baking dish. Mix soy sauce, ginger and sweet chili sauce in bowl, then slowly pour over fish. Spread onions around fish and sprinkle with salt and pepper. Bake for about 15 minutes until salmon is fully cooked. Serve with white rice.

Ginger Salmon Cakes

Serves 4

The sockeye is one of the most distinctive looking of the five species of Pacific salmon. Sockeye range in size from 5 to 7 pounds (2.3 to 3.2 kilograms). The sockeye salmon run in British Columbia's Fraser River reached record levels in August 2010. An estimated 30 million fish made their way up the Fraser, rivalling the historic salmon run of 1913. Since sockeye numbers had previously been on a downward trend, this new bumper crop came as welcome news to fisheries managers and anglers alike. The sockeye run was so extraordinary that the Pacific Salmon Commission even pressured the Department of Fisheries and Oceans to loosen the salmon harvest restrictions to allow a greater number of fish to be taken.

2 Tbsp (30 mL) coarsely chopped ginger
2 green onions, coarsely chopped
1 lb (454 g) boneless salmon fillet, skin removed
1 tsp (5 mL) cornstarch
1 egg white
pinch of salt
1 tsp (5 mL) Thai fish sauce

1 Tbsp (15 mL) canola oil
1 Tbsp (15 mL) sesame seeds
soy sauce, for serving
hot pepper sauce, for serving
1 lemon or lime, cut into wedges

In food processor, process ginger and green onions until finely chopped. Sprinkle salmon pieces with cornstarch and add to processor with egg white, salt and fish sauce. Using quick pulses, process until mixture resembles coarsely ground meat. Do not over-process.

Divide salmon mixture into 8 equal portions. Gently shape portions into patties about 1/2 inch (12 mm) thick. Transfer to plate, cover with plastic wrap and refrigerate for 5 to 10 minutes.

In large frying pan over medium, heat oil. Add salmon cakes and cook for about 3 minutes, until golden brown on first side. Turn cakes, adding more oil if needed, and cook for 2 to 3 minutes until cakes are slightly springy to the touch and have lost their raw colour in centre. Transfer to plates; sprinkle with sesame seeds. Serve with soy sauce, hot pepper sauce and lemon wedges.

Grilled Salmon with Dill

(*see* photo p. 88)

Serves 6

Campbell River, British Columbia, is known as Canada's salmon fishing capital. My father and I spent a couple of days on the water planning to land one of the river's fabled Tyee— a chinook salmon tipping the scales at 30 pounds (13.6 kilograms) or more. Although it never quite happened, our "cut plug" fishing presentation managed to entice a couple of spunky coho of 5 pounds (2.3 kilograms) or so apiece. For a small price, the Campbell River marina staff had our catch smoked and canned for us to bring home.

1/4 cup (60 mL) mayonnaise
1 Tbsp (15 mL) plain yogurt
2 tsp (10 mL) mustard seeds
1 1/2 tsp (7 mL) ground cumin
1/2 cup (125 mL) chopped fresh dill
3/4 tsp (4 mL) salt
1 Tbsp (15 mL) lemon juice
6 salmon steaks

Preheat grill to medium. Combine mayonnaise, yogurt, mustard seeds, cumin, dill, salt and lemon juice in large bowl. Spread mixture over salmon steaks, making sure to cover completely. Grill salmon for 7 to 8 minutes, turning once, until salmon meat separates easily from bone. Serve hot.

Try with This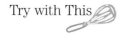

Herbed Cherry Tomatoes

Serves 6

3 cups (750 mL) cherry tomatoes, washed and drained
2 Tbsp (30 mL) olive oil
1 medium onion, minced
1 to 2 garlic cloves, finely chopped
1/2 cup (125 mL) soft breadcrumbs
1/4 cup (60 mL) chopped fresh parsley
1/2 tsp (2 mL) thyme
1/4 tsp (1 mL) salt
1/8 tsp (0.5 mL) pepper

Preheat oven to 400°F (205°C). Butter medium baking dish and place tomatoes in it. In small frying pan over medium-high, heat oil and sauté onion and garlic for 1 to 2 minutes. Add breadcrumbs and continue to sauté for 1 to 2 minutes. Remove from heat and add parsley, thyme, salt and pepper. Mix well and spoon over tomatoes. Bake for about 10 minutes until tomatoes are hot.

Stuffed Ouananiche

Serves 4

Atlantic salmon are closely tied to the tributaries connected to the Atlantic Ocean, though in recent years they have also been introduced into the Great Lakes with some success. Atlantics vary considerably from their Pacific cousins, possessing traits and characteristics closer to that of a trout. Atlantic salmon enter their birth rivers in eastern Canada during October and November to spawn. They do not die after spawning and may even return again to spawn in following years, though this phenomenon is quite rare. Some Atlantic salmon are landlocked and never leave their lake. These fish are called *ouananiche* and are found in Québec and parts of eastern Canada.

> 2 Tbsp (30 mL) butter
> 1 cup (250 mL) sliced mushrooms
> 2 shallots, sliced
> 2 garlic cloves, minced
> 1 1/2 cups (375 mL) breadcrumbs
> 4 slices bacon, cooked and crumbled
> 1/2 tsp (2 mL) pepper
> 1 × 2 to 3 lb (900 g to 1.4 kg) Atlantic salmon, cleaned (*see* p. 5), with head and tail removed
>
> salt and pepper, to taste
> 4 lemon wedges, for garnish

Preheat oven to 400°F (205°C). Grease baking pan; set aside. Heat butter in medium skillet and sauté mushrooms, shallots and garlic. Mix in breadcrumbs, bacon and pepper.

Press mixture into salmon cavity and season fish with salt and pepper. Place stuffed fish in prepared baking pan. Bake, covered, for about 30 minutes, then uncovered for another 10 minutes until fish flakes with a fork. Serve with lemon wedges.

Northern Québec Pike Fry (p. 79)

Grilled Salmon with Dill and
Herbed Cherry Tomatoes (p. 85)

Salmon Penne

Serves 4

Of all the rivers in Canada, Newfoundland's Gander River is, for me, the most memorable. Atlantic salmon fishing is a tradition on the Rock, and the Gander is one of the island's most popular destinations. I must point out that it is not for the faint of heart, and learning to fly-fish in hip waders is not an easy task. While fishing the Gander in my teen years, I learned the meaning of the saying "discretion is the better part of valour." While wading toward a better fishing spot on the river, I lost my footing and fell, instantly filling my waders with ice-cold water. If not for my father there to pull me to safety, I would be "swimming with the fishes" as they say! After that, I practised my fly-fishing a lot closer to shore.

> 2 cups (500 mL) sour cream
> 2 tsp (10 mL) dried dill
> 4 cups (1 L) penne pasta, uncooked
>
> 1 Tbsp (15 mL) extra-virgin olive oil
> 1 × 12 oz (340 g) boneless salmon fillet, skinned
> 1/2 tsp (2 mL) pepper
> 1 red pepper, chopped
> 2 shallots, sliced

Mix sour cream and dill in small bowl and set aside. Cook pasta according to package directions. Drain and keep warm.

Heat oil in large skillet and add salmon. Sprinkle fillet with pepper and cook for 5 minutes, turning several times. Once salmon is cooked, break into bite-sized pieces with end of spatula. Add red pepper and shallots to skillet, and cook for another 3 to 4 minutes until vegetables soften.

Reduce heat to low. Add pasta to skillet and stir gently. Slowly pour in sour cream mixture. Simmer on low for 5 minutes until creamy. Serve immediately.

Salmon with Mango Salsa

Serves 4

The chinook salmon is referred to as "king" for good reason. It is the largest and fastest-growing of all the salmon species by quite some margin. In the Pacific Northwest, where the chinook salmon grows the largest, it is not uncommon to see fish in the 30, 40 and even 50 pound (13.5 to 22.5 kilogram) range pulled in by sport fishermen. When you are this big, they call you king!

1 mango, peeled and diced
1/4 cup (60 mL) chopped spring onion (green part only)
1/4 cup (60 mL) diced red pepper
1 Tbsp (15 mL) finely diced fresh jalapeño pepper
1 garlic clove, minced
1 tsp (5 mL) lemon juice
1/4 tsp (1 mL) salt

2 large salmon fillets
lemon wedges, for garnish

For salsa, toss all ingredients except salmon together in bowl and stir. Place in refrigerator for 2 hours prior to serving.

Preheat oven to 375°F (190°C). On baking pan, bake salmon for 15 to 20 minutes until fish flakes easily with a fork. Separate fillets into 4 equal servings. Remove salsa from fridge and spread on salmon fillets. Garnish with lemon wedges.

Try with This 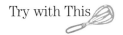 **French-fried Potatoes**

Serves 2

2/3 cup (150 mL) white sugar
2 cups (500 mL) warm water
2 large potatoes, peeled and sliced into 1/4-inch (6 mm) strips
6 cups (1.5 L) vegetable oil
salt, to taste

Put sugar and warm water in medium bowl and stir to dissolve sugar. Add potato strips and soak for about 15 minutes.

Place oil in deep-fryer and preheat to 375°F (190°C). Remove potato strips from water and dry thoroughly on paper towels. Discard water.

Fry potatoes in batches until golden, returning deep-fryer to 375°F (190°C) before adding each new batch. Drain on paper towels and season with salt.

Poached Salmon with Julienned Vegetables

(*see* photo p. 105)

Serves 4

When purchasing salmon from the fish market, you should be aware of the difference between wild salmon and farmed salmon. Farm-raised salmon contain unknown levels of cancer-causing PCBs, which are stored in the fish's fat layer. Wild salmon, on the other hand, generally contain little to no PCBs, depending on the water body they are from. Salmon absorb these harmful PCBs from the forage fish they feed on, as well as what has leached from contaminated soils. Farm-raised salmon are also sometimes coloured artificially to give them the classic pink salmon colour. Although mercury is occasionally found in wild salmon, mercury levels found in farmed salmon tend to be higher. I'm not saying that farmed salmon aren't fit for consumption, just that we should limit the number of farmed salmon meals we have per month.

1 Tbsp (15 mL) butter
1/2 celery rib, julienned
1/2 green pepper, julienned
1/2 red pepper, julienned
1/2 tsp (2 mL) fennel seed
1/2 tsp (2 mL) chopped fresh parsley

3 cups (750 mL) water
1/2 cup (125 mL) dry white wine
salt and pepper, to taste
4 × 8 oz (225 g) salmon steaks

juice from 1 lemon, for sprinkling

Heat butter in skillet over low. Add celery, green pepper, red pepper, fennel seed and parsley. Cook, covered, for 3 minutes; remove vegetable mixture from skillet and set aside.

Add water and wine to same skillet. Season with salt and pepper, and bring to a boil. Place salmon steaks in skillet; simmer for 6 minutes over low, turning once. Add julienned vegetables to skillet and cook for another 2 minutes until salmon feels firm.

Transfer salmon and vegetables to serving plates; sprinkle with lemon juice.

Moroccan Fish Steaks

Serves 4

Of all the Pacific salmon species we have in this country, chum may be the least well known; however, they are some of the most determined fish in Canada. Many of these special fish are proud residents of the Yukon. The majority of these chum salmon travel several thousand kilometres up the mighty Yukon River to spawn in small tributaries. Chum are what you might call "late bloomers" and are the last salmon to spawn in the fall, usually from November to late January. Chum will generally die about two weeks after they return to fresh water.

> 4 × 1-inch-thick (2.5 cm) salmon steaks
> 1 Tbsp (15 mL) coriander seed
> 1 Tbsp (15 mL) cumin seed
> 1 Tbsp (15 mL) caraway seed
> 1 Tbsp (15 mL) fennel seed
> 1/4 cup (60 mL) olive oil
> 2 tsp (10 mL) curry powder
> 3 tsp (15 mL) liquid honey
>
> 1 lemon, sliced

Place steaks in small baking dish. Mix coriander, cumin, caraway and fennel seeds together and grind slightly. Stir oil with ground seeds, curry powder and honey. Spread over both sides of fish. Cover baking dish and refrigerate overnight.

Preheat grill to medium and coat grill with oil or spray with non-stick spray. Remove salmon from fridge and place carefully on hot grill. Cook until outside of salmon is golden brown and inside flakes easily with a fork. Garnish with lemon slices and serve with French-fried Potatoes, p. 90, or Canadian Tea Biscuits, p. 16.

Pacific Salmon Stew

Serves 4

Many of the First Nations of western Canada have myths and legends involving salmon. In one story, a chief was so attached to his daughter that he did not want her to leave home. He understood that eventually she would have to leave, so in preparation for that day, the chief set up a special contest in her honour. His challenge was to see who could break the antlers off a deer. A nearby snail, squirrel, otter, beaver, wolf, bear and even a panther tried, but none of them could manage to break the antlers. After repeated taunts, a strange new creature appeared. It rose up, shook itself and, as the story goes, became whole and clean and very good to look upon. The people discovered the creature to be a salmon, which was victorious. We don't quite know what happened to the chief's daughter, as it was not part of the story, but we do know that a sneaky salmon beat out all other challengers.

2 cups (500 mL) fish stock (*see* Tip, p. 97)
1 lb (454 g) potatoes, boiled until soft, then cubed
1 1/4 cups (300 mL) mixed frozen vegetables (any variety)

1 Tbsp (15 mL) extra-virgin olive oil
1 onion, chopped
1 garlic clove, minced
1 lb (454 g) Pacific salmon fillet
salt and pepper, to taste

fresh bread or baguette

In large saucepan, bring fish stock to a boil. Add potatoes and mixed vegetables; simmer for 5 minutes. Set aside.

Meanwhile, in large, steep-sided skillet, heat olive oil. Sauté onion and garlic until tender. Season salmon with salt and pepper. Place salmon in skillet and cook for 8 minutes, turning once, until fish flakes with a fork. Break salmon into pieces with spatula.

Add salmon pieces and onion mixture to saucepan and mix well with potatoes and vegetables. Cover and simmer for 10 to 15 minutes on low. Serve with fresh bread or baguette.

Hot and Spicy Smelt

Serves 4

Smelt are a small schooling fish found across Canada and, according to experts, they are underutilized as a table fish. As with salmon and trout, smelt are loaded with omega-3s and are quite easy to prepare and serve. Because they are small, smelt are easily deep-fried or pan-fried and are one of the few fish you can eat whole without much of a problem. Most people prefer removing the heads, but when cooked properly, the rest of the smelt bones do not need to be discarded. Frozen smelt are available at most grocery stores. As a rule of thumb, 10 to 12 smelt will serve one person as a main course, and perhaps 4 to 5 as an appetizer. Although they are small, smelt are loaded with big taste!

1 lb (454 g) smelt, cleaned (*see* p. 5)
1 tsp (5 mL) turmeric, *divided*
salt, to taste
3/4 cup (175 mL) vegetable oil, *divided*

1 medium onion, finely chopped
2 medium potatoes, cut into wedges
1 Tbsp (15 mL) ginger-garlic paste
1 tsp (5 mL) red chili powder
1/2 tsp (2 mL) cumin powder
green chilies (optional)
1/2 cup (125 mL) water

In large bowl, toss fish with 1/2 tsp (2 mL) turmeric and salt. Heat 1/2 cup (125 mL) oil in frying pan and deep-fry fish. Remove to paper towels to drain; set aside.

Heat 1/4 cup (60 mL) oil in frying pan. Fry onion until golden brown. Add potatoes and fry for 5 minutes. Add ginger-garlic paste, 1/2 tsp (2 mL) turmeric, chili powder and cumin powder. Fry over medium until oil starts spitting. Add fried fish and fry for 5 minutes. For extra heat, add some green chilies. Add water and bring to a boil. Simmer for 10 minutes. Serve hot with rice.

Lake Erie Smelt

Serves 6

The first zebra mussels discovered in Canada were found in Lake St. Clair, a small water body connected to Lake Erie. It was 1988 and the dreaded mussels had found their way into the Great Lakes. They spread rapidly through the Great Lakes system by attaching onto watercraft. Zebra mussels have caused serious ecological damage over the past 20 years. They filter out phytoplankton and compete with many types of zooplankton, an important food source for young fish. What has resulted now is gin-clear water in the once-productive areas of Lake Erie. Although resident fish species have learned to adapt to the change in water clarity, the full impact of the zebra mussel infestation may never be known.

> 1/2 cup (125 mL) flour
> 1/2 tsp (2 mL) salt
> 1/4 tsp (1 mL) pepper
> 1 egg
> 1 Tbsp (15 mL) lemon juice
> 1/2 cup (125 mL) cracker crumbs
> 1/3 cup (75 mL) grated Parmesan cheese
> 2 lbs (900 g) smelt, cleaned and bones removed
>
> 1/2 cup (125 mL) canola or peanut oil, for frying

Mix flour, salt and pepper on plate. Beat egg and lemon juice in bowl. Mix cracker crumbs and Parmesan cheese on separate plate. Coat fish with flour mixture. Dip fish in egg mixture, then roll in cracker crumb mixture.

Heat about 1/4 inch (6 mm) canola or peanut oil in skillet. Pan-fry fish. When golden brown on one side, turn and brown other side. Serve hot.

Baked Sturgeon Fillets

Serves 4

Sturgeon fishing is tightly controlled in Canada. Heavy harvests prior to 1940 caused sturgeon populations across the country to nearly disappear. Since that time, fishing closures in many provinces have helped populations recover enough to support a sport fishery under very tight regulations. Québec is one of the few provinces that does allow for one sturgeon to be kept per person. Most sturgeon seasons in Canada are catch-and-release only, and sturgeon are showing signs of recovery. The sturgeon of the Fraser River, for example, appear to be doing very well under fairly moderate fishing pressure. In July and September 2012, two massive sturgeon were caught-and-released on separate occasions in the Fraser River, each weighing close to 1100 pounds (500 kilograms) and measuring nearly 13 feet (4 metres) long.

> 1 1/2 lbs (680 g) sturgeon fillets
> 1 cup (250 mL) sour cream
> 1 tsp (5 mL) lemon juice
> 1/3 cup (75 mL) grated Parmesan cheese
> 1 Tbsp (15 mL) chopped shallots
> 1/2 tsp (2 mL) pepper
> 1/2 tsp (2 mL) paprika

Preheat oven to 375°F (190°C). Place sturgeon fillets in greased shallow baking pan. In bowl, combine sour cream, lemon juice, Parmesan cheese, shallots and pepper. Spread over fillets and add dash of paprika. Bake, uncovered, for about 30 minutes until fish flakes with a fork. Serve hot with Garlic Couscous, p. 164, or Barb's Macaroni Salad, p. 165.

Sturgeon with Ginger

Serves 4

Sturgeon caviar was at one time the "be all and end all" snack for the rich and famous, until the Convention on International Trade in Endangered Species of Wild Fauna and Flora (CITES), a United Nations body, stopped nearly all legal export of this caviar worldwide. A group called the Endangered Fish Alliance— a Canadian coalition founded by chefs and conservationists aiming to teach the restaurant industry about sustainable alternatives—stepped in to promote farmed white sturgeon caviar, farmed paddlefish roe, farmed rainbow trout roe, whitefish roe and wild Pacific salmon roe. Even the expert palate has difficulty recognizing the difference among these *nouveau* alternative caviars.

2 tsp (10 mL) + 1 Tbsp (15 mL) butter, *divided*
4 × 2 oz (55 g) slices boneless sturgeon
salt and pepper, to taste

1 cup (250 mL) fish stock (*see* Tip)
1 × 1-inch (2.5 cm) piece ginger, peeled and finely chopped
3 garlic cloves, finely chopped
2/3 cup (150 mL) chopped tomato

Preheat oven to 350°F (175°C). Pound fish slices until they are evenly 1/8 inch (3 mm) thick.

Put 4 heat-resistant plates in oven until very hot. Remove hot plates and brush each with 1/2 tsp (2 mL) butter. Place piece of fish on each plate and season with salt and pepper. (The fish cooks on the hot plates while you make the sauce.)

Mix fish stock, ginger, garlic and tomato in saucepan and bring to a boil. Cook for 2 minutes. Whisk 1 Tbsp (15 mL) butter into sauce and pour over fish.

 tip MAKING FISH STOCK

Fish stock is easily made by covering the bones and heads of fish with cold water; add a quartered onion, a bay leaf, a garlic clove, a few peppercorns and thyme if you like; simmer but do not boil for 1 hour. Run through a fine-mesh sieve, allow to cool and freeze in sealable freezer bags.

Baked Crappie

Serves 4

Sunfish, you say? But aren't they too small for an adequate meal? Well, they may be small, but you would be making a mistake if you count them out when putting together a tasty fish meal. I will never forget a meal I had one time at a friend's house back home in Québec's beautiful Laurentians. The Provost family from my hometown had invited me to stay over for dinner and since they were serving fish—which I loved—I couldn't say no. The meal was absolutely unforgettable—and considering it was 30 years ago and I was 13 at the time, it must have been darn good. Once dinner was finished, I asked Madame Provost what type of fish we had just eaten and she replied, "Crapet-soleil." But it couldn't be, I thought, that is sunfish. As it turned out, it was most certainly a sunfish meal and perhaps one of the best I've ever had. The moral of the story is, don't count out sunfish, because they might very well be the best you've ever had!

> 10 to 12 crappie or pumpkinseed fillets
>
> 1 cup (250 mL) breadcrumbs or cornmeal
> 3/4 cup (175 mL) grated Parmesan cheese
> 1/4 cup (60 mL) chopped fresh or dried parsley
> 1 tsp (5 mL) salt
> 1/2 tsp (2 mL) pepper
> 1 tsp (5 mL) paprika
> 1/2 tsp (2 mL) fresh or dried oregano
>
> 1/2 cup (125 mL) melted butter
> lemon slices, for garnish

Preheat oven to 350°F (175°C). Rinse fish fillets and pat dry with paper towel. Mix breadcrumbs, Parmesan cheese, parsley, salt, pepper, paprika and oregano in bowl. Dip fillets in butter and coat with breadcrumb mixture. Place fish on non-stick baking sheet. Bake for about 30 minutes until fish flakes easily with a fork. Garnish with lemon slices.

Sunnies with Marjoram and Lemon Butter

Serves 4

With a trend in recent years away from recreational fishing, organizations are now encouraging young people to get involved in the sport. Perhaps the most important fish species in Canada, as far as youth fishing goes, is the sunfish or "sunnie." Children's fishing derbies and many National Fishing Week events usually involve sunfish. They are one of the most ubiquitous fish around, and are easy to catch under any fishing condition. For introducing young people to the sport, sunfish are ideal because they never tire of biting and can be caught on just about any bait. And since sunfish populations remain plentiful, they are a great starting point for any budding angler.

> 1 cup (250 mL) flour
> salt and pepper, to taste
> 4 sunfish, cleaned (*see* p. 5) and scaled (*see* Tip)
> 6 Tbsp (90 mL) butter
> 4 shallots or 3 garlic cloves, chopped
> 1/2 tsp (2 mL) dried marjoram
> 1 1/2 Tbsp (25 mL) lemon juice

Place flour, salt and pepper in small bowl. Place fish in flour mixture and turn to coat. Melt butter in skillet and add shallots or garlic, marjoram and fish. Cover pan and brown both sides of fish for about 5 minutes each side. Add lemon juice and cover pan. Over medium to low, cook fish about another 10 minutes.

To serve, pour some lemon butter from pan over each fish.

 SCALING A FISH

For scaling any fish, you require either a fillet knife with a long blade or a metal fish-scaling tool. Begin by placing your fish on a wooden cutting or fillet board. Hold the fish's head down firmly with your left hand and, with the knife in your right hand, begin scraping the fish "against the grain" from tail to head. The scales will loosen and fall off. Continue scraping until the side is smooth and scale-free. Turn the fish over and repeat with the other side. Rinse the fish under cool water to free any lingering scales before cooking.

Shallow-fried Crappie

Serves 4

According to the Northwest Ontario Sunset County Travel Association, fishing for crappie in that region of Ontario can, at times, seem like fishing in a barrel. They are not always easy to find, but when you do locate them, the action is lightning fast! Some of the best crappie opportunities are had through the ice or just after ice-out, when they move inshore to feed. In most cases, you'll find them in 20 to 40 feet (6 to 12 metres) of water or suspended along deep weed lines. To catch them with consistency, try using live minnows with a small jig. This popular panfish can be found in large numbers in certain lakes—a true delicacy that is considered one of the best fish to eat.

> 1 cup (250 mL) peanut or canola oil
> 1 tsp (5 mL) cayenne pepper
> 1/2 cup (125 mL) mustard
>
> 10 crappie fillets
> 2 cups (500 mL) all-purpose flour
>
> salt and pepper, to taste

In deep-sided skillet, heat oil. In small bowl, combine cayenne pepper and mustard. Set aside.

Roll up fillets and use toothpicks to hold in place. Brush mustard mixture on rolled-up fillets. Dip fillets in flour.

Place fillets in hot oil in skillet and cook until golden brown. Season with salt and pepper.

Sautéed Crappie

Serves 4

The black crappie is the most common type of crappie found in Canada and may live as long as 15 years, but 6 to 7 years is a more typical life span. The black crappie prefers clearer water than the white crappie, which may explain its prevalence in Canadian waters. Crappie propagation is a male-dominated activity since the male not only constructs the nest but also guards it from predators. Once the female has deposited her eggs, her work is done.

    1 cup (250 mL) butter
    2 cups (500 mL) chopped onion
    2 cups (500 mL) chopped celery
    1 cup (250 mL) chopped red pepper
    1 Tbsp (15 mL) flour
    1 cup (250 mL) chopped green onions (green part only)
    1 tsp (5 mL) soy sauce

    2 lbs (900 g) crappie fillets
    1/2 tsp (2 mL) salt
    1/2 tsp (2 mL) pepper

In skillet, melt butter and add onion, celery and red pepper; sauté until softened. Add flour and stir to combine. Add green onions and soy sauce. Stir well.

Place fillets in skillet and cover with sauce. Simmer for about 10 minutes until fish flakes easily with a fork. Season with salt and pepper.

Bluegill Sauté

Serves 4

Bluegill may be small in stature, but what they lack in size, they more than make up for in taste. They can be filleted in the same way as a bass or crappie, with one fillet removed from each side. Your beautiful bluegill may just be the most delectable fish you've ever eaten.

    1 cup (250 mL) flour
    1/2 tsp (2 mL) salt
    1/2 tsp (2 mL) pepper
    12 bluegill fillets
    4 Tbsp (60 mL) butter

    1 tsp (5 mL) lemon juice
    1 tsp (5 mL) chopped parsley
    1 lemon, cut into slices

In medium mixing bowl, combine flour, salt and pepper. Dredge bluegill fillets in flour. In large skillet over medium, melt butter and fry fillets until golden brown.

Once nearly cooked, add lemon juice and chopped parsley. Continue to sauté for 2 to 3 minutes until parsley softens. Garnish with lemon slices and serve.

Stuffed Baked Brookies

Serves 4

The many different species of trout in Canada are extensive and wide-ranging but share one important common thread—a tiny little fin located between the pelvic fins and caudal known as the axillary process. As inconspicuous as it looks, this one small appendage separates them from all other fish. Trout, along with salmon, are members of the elite family Salmonidae. Trout species found in Canada include the king of the trout family, the lake trout, as well as brook trout (brookies), rainbow trout, brown trout and Dolly Varden and several hybrid species. Trout are considered by professional chefs and the general population alike to be one of the best-tasting fish this great country has to offer.

> 3 Tbsp (45 mL) olive oil
> 6 cups (1.5 L) sliced mushrooms
> 1 1/2 cups (375 mL) finely chopped onion
> 1 celery rib, finely chopped
> salt and pepper
>
> 4 brook trout, cleaned (*see* p. 5)
> 2 Tbsp (30 mL) lemon juice
> 1/4 cup (60 mL) melted butter

In cast-iron skillet, heat olive oil, then add mushrooms, onion and celery. Fry, stirring occasionally, until mushrooms brown and oil has been absorbed. Remove from heat. Season with salt and pepper; set aside.

Preheat oven to 350°F (175°C). Coat baking sheet with non-stick cooking spray. Fill trout cavities with mushroom mixture, and sprinkle with lemon juice. Brush trout with butter and lay on baking sheet. Bake trout for 15 minutes until golden brown and fish separates easily from bone. Serve immediately.

Traditional Pan-seared Trout

Serves 6

Brook trout, with their brilliant colour and bright speckled skin, have often been considered one of the most aesthetically pleasing of all fish. The brookie or speckled, as they are often called, are downright pretty, and boy do they carry their speckles with pride. Brookies are found in a variety of coldwater Canadian lakes with gravelly tributaries and spring upwellings, and are often pursued by fly fishermen in the springtime. Pound for pound, the brook trout is also said to be one of the hardest-fighting sport fish in the world. They may reach a maximum size of perhaps 5 to 6 pounds (2.2 to 2.7 kilograms) depending on the water body and generally live only 7 to 8 years in the wild.

> 1/2 cup (125 mL) cornmeal or breadcrumbs
> 1/4 cup (60 mL) flour
> salt and pepper, to taste
> 1 egg
> 1/3 cup (75 mL) milk
> 2 × 3/4 lb (340 g) brook trout (12 to 14 inches each),
>   cleaned (*see* p. 5), with heads removed
> 4 Tbsp (60 mL) butter
> 1 lemon, sliced

In large mixing bowl, whisk together cornmeal, flour, salt and pepper. In second bowl, mix egg and milk together. Pat trout dry with paper towel. Roll trout in cornmeal mixture, then in milk mixture and then again in cornmeal mixture.

Heat butter in hot skillet or cast-iron frying pan. Cook trout in pan, flipping once, until brown. Then lower heat, cover and let simmer for 4 minutes. Serve garnished with lemon slices.

 tip **REMOVING BACKBONES**

To remove backbones from fish, you will need a sharp fillet knife and a steady hand. Start by making a small, shallow incision down through the back of the fish, starting from the front and continuing all the way to the tail. Once the backbone is exposed, skin down each side of the spine about 1/4 inch (6 mm) with the tip of your fillet knife, making sure not to cut through the bone. When both sides of the fish are skinned down and the spine is exposed, cut through the rib cage from front to back with a cross motion. Discard the spine and close the fish back up.

Campfire Smoked Trout

Serves 6

Rainbow trout are easily one of this country's most popular wild fish served as table fare. They are versatile too, and raised extensively in fish hatcheries across the country for stocking purposes. Fresh rainbow trout can be found in almost every fish store and corner grocery store. They are a challenging fish to catch because of their sometimes finicky nature, but their pink flesh and mild taste make them an ideal choice for a multitude of wild fish recipes. Although most rainbow trout are land-locked, living in the clear coldwater lakes of the Canadian Shield, others are migratory and travel tributaries to spawn each spring. These migratory spring spawners are called "steelhead" in western Canada and around the Great Lakes.

> **2 cups (500 mL) water**
> **juice from 1 lemon, plus more for drizzling**
> **5 garlic cloves, sliced**
> **4 shallots, sliced**
> **2 Tbsp (30 mL) salt**
> **2 Tbsp (30 mL) sugar**
> **2 Tbsp (30 mL) chopped dill**
> **6 boneless rainbow trout (10 to 12 inches),**
> **   backbone, ribs and tail removed (*see* Tip, p. 103)**
>
> **2 Tbsp (30 mL) horseradish, or to taste**

In bowl, combine water, lemon juice, garlic, shallots, salt, sugar and dill. Place trout in large glass baking dish and pour marinade over top. Refrigerate for 4 to 5 hours.

Meanwhile, soak wood chips in water for a few hours (*see* p. 11 for types of wood and smoking techniques). Build charcoal or briquette fire on one side of grill and place shallow pan of water on other half. When coals are hot, begin to scatter wet wood chips on top of coals, which will produce large billows of smoke. Place trout on grill over pan of water, and then put lid or cover over grill to trap smoke inside. Cook for about 30 minutes until meat flakes easily with a fork.

Serve trout drizzled with lemon juice and horseradish.

 tip   Marinate fish before hitting the woods.

Poached Salmon with Julienned Vegetables (p. 91)

Tequila Trout with Salsa Fresca (p. 107)
Vegetable Rice (p. 45)

Tequila Trout with Salsa Fresca

(*see* photo p. 106)

Serves 6

Brook trout, or speckled trout as they are commonly called, can be found throughout hundreds of coldwater streams and lakes across the Canadian Shield. Brookies are known for their wonderful spawning colours come fall. The male brook develops a pronounced "hooked" lower jaw known as a kipe. The male will also turn a brilliant red, which is believed to be for attracting females. Whatever the case, the spawning colour is something to behold.

6 ripe plum tomatoes, diced
1 onion, diced
1 jalapeño pepper, seeded and minced
2 Tbsp (30 mL) chopped cilantro
1 Tbsp (15 mL) lime juice
1 Tbsp (15 mL) cumin powder
1 Tbsp (15 mL) garlic powder
7 Tbsp (105 mL) tequila, *divided*
1 tsp (5 mL) salt
1 tsp (5 mL) pepper

2 Tbsp (30 mL) vegetable oil
6 × 6 oz (170 g) trout fillets
chili powder, to taste
lemon pepper, to taste
dried dill, to taste

1 Tbsp (15 mL) chopped cilantro, for garnish

For salsa, mix tomatoes, onion, jalapeño pepper, cilantro, lime juice, cumin powder, garlic powder, 1 Tbsp (15 mL) tequila, salt and pepper in processor. Pulse briefly a few times for chunky texture. Transfer to bowl and refrigerate.

In large skillet, heat oil over medium-high until barely smoking. Sprinkle fillets with chili powder, lemon pepper and dill, and cook for 5 to 7 minutes, turning once, until golden brown and flake easily when tested with a fork.

Remove pan from heat and splash 1 Tbsp (15 mL) tequila on each fillet. Carefully ignite tequila with match or lighter. Shake pan gently until flames subside. Transfer to individual plates. Top with salsa and garnish with cilantro.

Asian Honey Lake Trout

Serves 4

Lake trout are the epitome of the deep-dwelling freshwater fish. Of all the land-locked members of the trout and salmon family Salmonidae, the lake trout is the most coldwater-loving of them all. During the spring, after ice-out, "lakers" can been found cruising the shallows in search of a quick meal. It is the one time of year when fishermen can catch lake trout without the use of specialized equipment. As soon as summer arrives and water temperatures begin to rise, lake trout begin their descent into deep water, often more than 100 feet (30 metres) below the surface.

> 4 × 10 to 12 oz (280 to 340 g) trout fillets
> 1 × 8 oz (227 mL) can crushed pineapple, drained
> 1/3 cup (75 mL) chopped onion
> 1/4 cup (60 mL) honey
> 3 Tbsp (45 mL) soy sauce
> 2 Tbsp (30 mL) hoisin sauce
> 2 Tbsp (30 mL) lime juice
> 2 Tbsp (30 mL) white wine
> 2 tsp (10 mL) peeled and grated fresh ginger
> 1 1/2 tsp (7 mL) cornstarch
> 2 jalapeño peppers, finely chopped
> 1 garlic clove, chopped

Preheat oven to 425°F (220°C). Grease baking dish and place fish in it. Mix remaining ingredients in bowl and pour over fish. Bake for 15 minutes until fish flakes easily with a fork.

Try with This  ## Sweet Canadian Marinade
Makes 1/2 cup (125 mL)

1/4 cup (60 mL) pure Canadian maple syrup
2 Tbsp (30 mL) Dijon mustard
2 garlic cloves, minced
1 Tbsp (15 mL) balsamic vinegar
1 tsp (5 mL) salt
1/2 tsp (2 mL) pepper

Combine ingredients and mix well. Chill for 2 to 3 hours. Use as marinade or brush on any fish.

Smoky Trout Burgers

(see photo p. 123)

Serves 4

The migratory rainbow trout or steelhead is forever the subject of great discussion among fishermen. Steelhead spawn in lake tributaries during the early spring and return to the lake following spring migration. Since they almost completely stop feeding during the spring run, catching them on hook and line is a challenge for even the most accomplished angler. Fish roe bags or egg sacks are the most commonly used bait, along with light line and a long, tapered pole known as a noodle rod. Fishermen catch steelhead by allowing their roe bags to drift naturally down the river in the hope that a shiny migratory trout will pick it up.

2 potatoes, cut into chunks
12 oz (340 g) smoked trout fillets, flaked
2 tsp (10 mL) creamed horseradish
6 shallots, finely chopped
3/4 cup (175 mL) grated zucchini, squeezed dry
salt and pepper, to taste

2 Tbsp (30 mL) flour
8 lean bacon slices

Boil potatoes in lightly salted water until cooked. Drain, mash and transfer to large bowl. Add trout, horseradish, shallots, zucchini, salt and pepper; mix well. Separate mixture into 4 equal portions and form into patties. Refrigerate for 1 hour.

Preheat barbecue to medium-high. Dredge patties in flour and wrap each in 2 slices of bacon. Grill for 3 to 4 minutes on each side until golden.

Try with This  **Baked Sweet Potato Fries**

Serves 4

1 lb (454 g) sweet potatoes, scrubbed
1 Tbsp (15 mL) melted butter
1/4 tsp (1 mL) seasoning salt
1/4 tsp (1 mL) ground nutmeg

Preheat oven to 450°F (230°C) and spray large, shallow baking pan or rimmed baking sheet with non-stick cooking spray. Cut potatoes lengthwise into quarters, and then cut each quarter into 2 wedges. Arrange in pan in single layer. Combine butter, salt and nutmeg in bowl and brush on potatoes. Bake for 20 minutes until brown and tender.

Brook Trout Sauté

Serves 2

The average brook trout caught in the Canadian wild ranges from 10 to 12 inches (25 to 30 centimetres) long and weighs about 1/2 pound (0.2 kilograms). In many of the more remote waters, brookies can grow to 20 inches (50 centimetres) or more and weigh in excess of 5 pounds (2.3 kilograms). Always keep in mind the wide range in size when cooking the elusive brook trout. Because of their small average size, it is uncommon for brook trout to be filleted, and small, pan-sized brookies may even be consumed bones and all. When frying larger brook trout, be sure to remove the head and tail and leave the skin intact. Trout skin is very thin and mild tasting with no scales and can be eaten along with the rest of the fish.

3 Tbsp (45 mL) olive oil
2 shallots, thinly sliced
1 garlic clove, sliced

2 cups (500 mL) white wine, *divided*
1/2 tsp (2 mL) dried thyme
salt and pepper

2 × 10 to 14 inch (25 to 35 cm) brook trout,
    cleaned (*see* p. 5), with heads and tails removed

Heat oil in medium skillet. Add shallots and garlic and cook for 10 minutes. Increase heat and add 1 cup (250 mL) wine; cook until reduced to syrupy consistency. Add 1 cup (250 mL) wine, thyme, salt and pepper; let simmer for 4 minutes over medium.

Remove pan from heat, then add trout. Allow trout to simmer for only a few minutes. Do not turn fish but baste with surrounding liquid with a spoon. Cook until fish flakes easily with a fork. Remove fillets to serving plates and serve immediately.

Roasted Lake Trout

Serves 4

Lake trout are the largest and longest-living member of the trout family. However, their growth rate varies greatly with the environment they inhabit. Lake trout living in southern Canada—in the Great Lakes, for example—tend to grow quickly but do not live as long. Lakers in the Northwest Territories' Great Bear Lake, by contrast, have a greater life expectancy and grow much more slowly. Lake trout also have a different overall appearance depending on what region they hail from. Lakers from the cold water of northern Canada tend to be quite "front heavy," with very large heads and more streamlined bodies. Lake trout from the south, on the other hand, have smaller heads and a much larger midsection.

1/3 cup (75 mL) lemon juice
1 Tbsp (15 mL) olive oil
1 Tbsp (15 mL) chopped parsley
1/4 tsp (1 mL) thyme
1/8 tsp (0.5 mL) pepper
1 lb (454 g) boneless lake trout fillets

1 lemon, sliced

Combine lemon juice, oil, parsley, thyme and pepper together in mixing bowl. Add fillets, making sure they are completely covered in mixture. Refrigerate for 1 to 2 hours.

Preheat oven to 400°F (205°C). Remove fillets from bowl with tongs and place on non-stick baking dish. Roast on top oven rack for 10 to 15 minutes until fish flakes easily with a fork. Garnish with lemon slices and serve.

Try with This  **Lemon Sauce**

Makes 3/4 cup (175 mL)

1/2 cup (125 mL) butter
2 Tbsp (30 mL) lemon juice
2 Tbsp (30 mL) fish stock (*see* Tip, p. 97)
lemon wedges

Combine butter, juice and stock in small saucepan, and bring to a boil. Serve over cooked trout. Garnish with lemon wedges.

Trout with Tahini Sauce

Serves 4

The biggest concern most people have with preparing a fish meal is the time required to clean or fillet the fish, and then having to line up the ingredients and study the directions to hopefully get everything spot-on. This trout recipe has all your bases covered, with ease of preparation and lightning-fast delivery time from start to finish. In 10 short minutes, your trout with tahini is on the table, piping hot and ready to serve. Not only is it fast, but you may also substitute any type of trout—for example, you might prefer brookies over rainbows. Whatever trout you get your hands on will work with this dish, and then all you'll need to do is dig in and enjoy!

4 × 6 oz (170 g) rainbow or brown trout fillets
1/4 tsp (1 mL) salt
1/4 tsp (1 mL) pepper

1/3 cup (75 mL) plain yogurt
2 Tbsp (30 mL) tahini
2 Tbsp (30 mL) mayonnaise
1 Tbsp (15 mL) lemon juice
1 garlic clove, minced
1 tsp (5 mL) chopped green onion
1 tsp (5 mL) chopped fresh parsley
pinch of salt
pinch of pepper
pinch of cayenne pepper

Preheat grill to medium-high. Season trout with salt and pepper. Place fish, skin side down, on greased grill; close lid and grill until fish flakes easily with a fork.

Meanwhile, combine all remaining ingredients in small bowl and mix with wire whisk. Serve fish drizzled with sauce.

Almond Lake Trout

Serves 4

The lake trout is a large, coldwater-dwelling member of the trout family. Perhaps the lake trout's biggest claim to fame is its ability to live for 40 years and even longer, especially in more northern regions. When keeping lake trout for consumption, it is important to use only the smaller fish as larger lakers that have spent many years in a given body of water will have accumulated toxins in their fat layers. Mercury will concentrate in the fish's fat layer with levels that increase gradually over time. Whenever keeping larger fish for consumption, remove all belly meat as the highest fat content is found in this part of the fish.

1/4 cup (60 mL) almonds, crumbled

1/4 cup (60 mL) butter
2 Tbsp (30 mL) chopped shallots
2 lbs (900 g) lake trout fillets
2 lemons, sliced and *divided*

Preheat oven to 300°F (150°C). Spread almonds on baking sheets and toast for about 15 minutes until slightly brown.

Preheat grill to medium. Melt butter in saucepan and add almonds and shallots. Stir until almonds are well coated, then transfer to bowl. Directly on grill, arrange fillets on top of half of lemon slices; grill, covered, for 3 to 4 minutes. Do not turn; fillets will turn opaque when done. Carefully remove fillets from grill and serve topped with almond mixture and garnished with remaining lemon slices.

Try with This  **Traditional Mashed Potatoes**

Serves 6

6 medium russet potatoes, peeled and cubed
1/2 cup (125 mL) warm milk
1/4 cup (60 mL) butter or margarine
3/4 tsp (4 mL) salt
1/4 tsp (1 mL) pepper

Boil potatoes in large pot of lightly salted water for 20 to 25 minutes until very tender. Drain well. Add milk, butter, salt and pepper. Mash with hand mixer until potatoes are light and fluffy. Serve immediately.

Stuffed Brook Trout

Serves 4

If ever there were a specimen worthy of the title "nature's perfect food," it would be the brook trout. Brookies are wide-ranging and readily available in hundreds of our freshwater streams and lakes. They tend to dwell in our country's coolest, clearest water. Brookies are as pure as mountain spring water and as mild and flavourful as anything you will ever eat. I consider them a Canadian icon destined for the dinner table. Thank you, Mother Nature, for the brook trout—this truly perfect food you have provided us.

> 4 × 10 oz (280 g) whole brook trout,
>   cleaned (*see* p. 5), with heads removed
> 3 garlic cloves, minced
> 1 onion, chopped
> 1 Tbsp (15 mL) lemon juice
> 2 Tbsp (30 mL) butter
> 1 1/2 tsp (7 mL) garlic powder
> salt and pepper, to taste
> 2 jalapeño peppers, diced

Preheat oven to 400°F (205°C). Fill each trout cavity with garlic and onion; sprinkle with lemon juice. Cover each trout with butter, and place on large piece of foil. Season with garlic powder, salt and pepper. Spread jalapeño peppers on top of fish. Cover fish over with foil and fold sides to make a tight seal. Bake trout for 30 minutes until meat is fluffy and separates easily from bone.

Mediterranean Trout

Serves 4

It may sound like a cliché, but I will never forget the day the big one got away. It was 1979 and I was fishing with my father on Québec's famous Lake Mistassini. Within minutes, I felt a tug on my line and set the hook. I knew I had a trout on, and by the weight of the hookset, it felt like a monster. For some unknown reason, though, this big "spec" made a beeline for the boat and I reeled like crazy to keep up. Within seconds, my line was wrapped around the outboard and my father tried frantically to free it. That's when he caught a glimpse of it—the largest brook trout he had ever laid eyes on! "It's way over 2 feet long!" he yelled, just as my line snapped and my once-in-a-lifetime trout swam off. That year, we caught a massive 8-pound (3.6 kilogram) brookie—our personal best—but Dad says my fish was considerably larger than that one. I am glad, at least, that I didn't see the big fish myself—it is a vision my father has to live with.

6 potatoes, diced

2 Tbsp (30 mL) extra-virgin olive oil
4 × 12 to 14 oz (340 to 400 g) trout fillets,
**   rinsed and patted dry**
salt and pepper, to taste

1 yellow pepper, thinly sliced
2 medium onions, thinly sliced
2 Tbsp (30 mL) chopped Greek olives
4 tomatoes, chopped
1 Tbsp (15 mL) capers, drained
2 Tbsp (30 mL) white wine

Place potatoes in pot with salted water; bring to a boil and cook until tender. Drain and set aside.

Heat oil in large skillet over medium. Season trout fillets with salt and pepper; cook in skillet for 10 minutes, turning once.

Spread yellow pepper and onions on trout and sauté for 5 minutes. Then sprinkle olives, tomatoes and capers on top of fillets. Add wine and simmer for 5 minutes. Serve trout and vegetables with boiled potatoes.

Beer-battered Walleye

(*see* photo p. 124)

Serves 8

The ubiquitous Beer-battered Walleye dish has been a Canadian favourite for years, as it blends two of the country's favourite pastimes: living off the fat of the land and, of course, beer drinking. In some parts of central Canada, this recipe is known as Beer-battered Pickerel, and in parts of Québec, it is called Beer-battered Doré. Whatever it's called, the end result is the same, with walleye being the single best fish choice in the beer-battered fish-fry circles. One of this country's most sought-after sport fish, the walleye is often called old marble eyes, golden perch or simply "eyes" by many anglers.

> **peanut or sunflower oil, for deep-frying**
> **3 1/3 cups (825 mL) flour, *divided***
> **1 3/4 tsp (9 mL) salt, plus extra for sprinkling**
> **1/2 tsp (2 mL) cayenne pepper**
> **2 × 12 oz (341 mL) bottles beer**
> **2 lbs (900 g) walleye fillets**

Place oil in deep-fryer to depth recommended by manufacturer and preheat to 370°F (188°C). Mix 3 cups (750 mL) flour, salt and cayenne pepper together in bowl, then whisk in beer until smooth in consistency. Place remaining flour on plate. Pat walleye fillets dry with paper towel, then dredge in flour, shaking off excess. Dip each fillet one by one into batter and then gently place in hot oil. Deep-fry until golder brown, turning only once. Use slotted spoon (never a fork!) to transfer fish to paper towel-lined plate. Sprinkle lightly with salt. Serve with Old-fashioned Onion Rings, p. 62.

 TESTING OIL TEMPERATURE

To test the temperature of your oil, try dropping in a single popping corn kernel. If the kernel pops within a few seconds, your temperature is at least 350°F (175°C). You can also dip the end of a wooden spoon into your oil—it begins bubbling around the wooden end when it is 350°F to 375°F (175°C to 190°C).

Blackened Walleye

Serves 2

Over the years, the noble walleye has been victim of what one might call a fish identity crisis. The walleye's smaller and less prevalent cousin, the sauger, has often been mistaken for walleye. In parts of Québec, where walleye take on a purplish-blue tinge, they are known as blue walleye. Since the original blue walleye of the Great Lake–St. Lawrence region are said to have become extinct over 50 years ago, the bluish colour of Québec's special walleye is believed to be from water colour and a specific algae in the lake water. Although scientists have yet to prove the existence of the old remnant blue walleye population elsewhere in Canada, residents of Québec remain convinced that these beautiful blue-coloured fish are one and the same. Regardless of their colour, distribution or name, the walleye remains one of this country's most important fish species.

6 to 8 small tomatoes, halved lengthwise and seeded
3 garlic cloves, minced
1/4 cup (60 mL) chopped fresh thyme
salt and pepper, to taste
1/2 cup (125 mL) extra-virgin olive oil

1 tsp (5 mL) salt
1 tsp (5 mL) pepper
1 tsp (5 mL) paprika
2 tsp (10 mL) chili powder
2 tsp (10 mL) ground cumin
2 tsp (10 mL) dried thyme
2 × 12 to 15 oz (340 to 425 g) fresh walleye,
    cleaned (*see* p. 5) but not filleted
2 Tbsp (30 mL) canola oil

Preheat oven to 250°F (120°C). Arrange tomatoes cut-side up in shallow roasting pan. Mix garlic, thyme, salt, pepper and oil in small bowl and drizzle over tomatoes. Bake for 3 hours until tomatoes are chewy.

Heat heavy skillet until smoking hot. In small bowl, mix salt, pepper, paprika, chili powder, cumin and thyme. Rinse fish and pat dry with paper towel. Brush fish with oil and rub with spice mixture. Cook fish for 3 to 4 minutes on each side until meat flakes easily with a fork. Transfer to serving platter and arrange dried tomatoes attractively on fish. Serve immediately.

Stuffed Walleye

Serves 4

When preparing bony fish like bass or walleye, you cannot do without a good-quality filleting knife, such as those by Rapala or Normark. The trick to using a filleting knife properly when cleaning fish is to think of it as an extension of your hand. Hold the knife as if you were shaking someone's hand, and extend your pointer finger down the blade shaft to offer a more controlled cut. A precisely sharpened knife will cut cleanly and smoothly through the fish's flesh without being so sharp as to slice right through the smaller bones. With some practice, you will become proficient at cleaning, filleting and boning any wild fish species—remember that it all begins with using the proper tools!

> 4 × 12 to 14 oz (240 to 400 g) walleye fillets
> 2 Tbsp (30 mL) melted butter
> juice from 1 lemon
> salt and pepper, to taste
> 1 white bread slice, crumbled
> 1 cup (250 mL) breadcrumbs
> 1/2 tsp (2 mL) parsley
> 1/2 tsp (2 mL) garlic powder
> 1 egg, beaten

Preheat oven to 350°F (175°C). Arrange walleye in baking dish. Brush fillets with butter and drizzle lemon juice over top. Sprinkle with salt and pepper. Combine crumbled bread, breadcrumbs, parsley, garlic powder, egg, salt and pepper. Form mixture into 4 clumps and place on top of each walleye fillet. Cover dish with foil and bake for about 10 minutes until fish flakes easily with a fork. Serve hot.

Gratin of Walleye

Serves 4

Walleye are one of this country's most highly sought-after game fish and can be found in every province and territory. They prefer cold, dark water and tend to be crepuscular feeders (they are more active in the early morning and late in the day). Walleye are also highly piscivorous—they feed almost exclusively on other fish species. With their large, distinctive marble eyes, walleye have learned to adapt to low-light conditions to find their prey. These light-sensitive creatures have a distinct advantage over other fish in their ability to live and feed in almost complete darkness.

2 green peppers

3 Tbsp (45 mL) canola oil
2 garlic cloves, finely chopped
2 lbs (900 g) walleye fillets, cut into 1-inch (2.5 cm) cubes
salt and pepper, to taste

2 Tbsp (30 mL) minced parsley
2 Tbsp (30 mL) minced capers, with juice
1/2 cup (125 mL) breadcrumbs
1/2 tsp (2 mL) dried thyme

Preheat broiler. Broil green peppers, turning them as skin turns black. Place peppers in paper bag and set aside to cool.

Heat oil in large frying pan. Add garlic and sauté until barely golden. Season walleye fillets with salt and pepper. Increase heat and add fish cubes to pan. Fry for about 5 minutes, stirring constantly. Remove from heat.

Pinch off blackened skin of peppers and cut peppers in half. Remove seeds and cut peppers into thin strips. Place strips in bowl; stir in parsley, capers, breadcrumbs and thyme.

Divide fish cubes into 4 gratin dishes; top with pepper mixture. Broil for about 1 minute to brown. Serve immediately.

Grilled Walleye with Tomato Relish

Serves 4

One pitfall many people find themselves in when cooking walleye (pickerel) is over-treating it. This fish is so mild that we must remember to never over-batter or over-season it. As with soul fish, heavy marinating or a thick tempura batter may easily overpower walleye. Most walleye recipes keep the fillet light and relatively unchanged since the fish has such a pleasant, mild flavour and texture. In the case of the pristine Canadian walleye, less is often more.

2 tsp (10 mL) ground coriander
1/2 tsp (2 mL) pepper
2 cups (500 mL) diced tomatoes
1/2 cup (125 mL) chopped cilantro
1 jalapeño pepper, seeded and minced
2 Tbsp (30 mL) chopped onion
2 Tbsp (30 mL) olive oil
2 Tbsp (30 mL) lime juice
1 1/2 tsp (7 mL) grated ginger root
1/2 tsp (2 mL) salt

2 lbs (900 g) walleye, cleaned (*see* p. 5) but not filleted
salt and pepper

For relish, heat coriander and pepper in small skillet over medium for about 2 minutes. Transfer to medium bowl and add tomatoes, cilantro, jalapeño pepper, onion, olive oil, lime juice, ginger and salt. Mix well, then set aside.

Preheat grill to medium-high. Open cavity of walleye and sprinkle inside with salt and pepper. Grill for 10 to 12 minutes, until meat flakes easily with a fork. Drizzle with relish and serve.

Honey-fried Walleye

Serves 4

In Canada, walleye differ greatly in colour and appearance depending on their environment. Walleye that dwell in dark, brackish water appear paler, with dark black patterns across their bodies. On the other hand, walleye that live in clear waters tend to be more vividly marked with olive to brown. What remains the same throughout this fish's range is the size and shape of their eyes, which are, after all, the walleye's namesake. All walleye have protruding eyes that are very large in relation to the size of their bodies. The walleye's eyes often exhibit a luminescent glow, a feature rarely found in other fish species. They come by their nickname "old marble eyes" honestly.

2 eggs
1 to 2 tsp (5 to 10 mL) liquid honey

1 to 1 1/2 cups (250 to 375 mL) medium crushed
    saltine crackers (about 20)
1/3 cup (75 mL) flour
1/4 tsp (1 mL) salt
1/4 tsp (1 mL) pepper
4 × 10 to 12 oz (280 to 340 g) boneless walleye fillets

vegetable or canola oil, for frying
lemon wedges, for garnish

In small bowl, beat eggs and honey until mixed. Place crackers in sealable plastic bag and close bag, releasing all air. Use rolling pin or meat mallet to crush crackers to medium-fine texture. Add flour, salt and pepper to cracker mixture and mix well. Pour some cracker mixture on plate, adding more as needed. Dip each fillet in egg mixture, then in cracker mixture.

Heat 1/4 inch (6 mm) oil in large skillet over medium. Place fillets in hot oil and fry for 3 to 4 minutes until fillets are golden and flake easily. Garnish with lemon and serve.

Ginger Walleye

Serves 8

The walleye, or pickerel as they are called in parts of Canada, are similar to trout in that they may be cooked with the skin on when the recipe calls for it, such as in this one. Although the skin is moderately thick, the scales are tiny and will not give the dish any unpleasant flavour or odour. Of course, when it comes to eating, the scales must be discarded. These days it is more common anyway to get walleye fillets with the skin on, because many provinces' fish and wildlife departments require filleted fish to retain their skin during transportation. Conservation or fisheries officers must be able to identify each fish species kept for consumption, a task which is nearly impossible without the presence of skin.

> 1 cup (250 mL) peeled and halved onions
> 2/3 cup (150 mL) cider vinegar
> 1/4 cup (60 mL) soy sauce
> 2 Tbsp (30 mL) olive oil
> 1/2 tsp (2 mL) thyme
> 6 thin slices ginger root
> 2 garlic cloves, minced
> 1/4 tsp (1 mL) pepper
>
> 2 lbs (900 g) boneless walleye fillets, skin on

Place all ingredients except fish in large skillet over medium-high and bring to a boil. Slice fish into 3- to 4-inch (7.5 to 10 cm) pieces, then add to skillet. Reduce heat and simmer for 10 minutes. Transfer fish to paper towel–lined serving platter.

Boil sauce until it has reduced to about 1/2 cup (125 mL), then drizzle over fillets and serve.

Smoky Trout Burgers and
Baked Sweet Potato Fries (p. 109)

Beer-battered Walleye (p. 116)
Old-fashioned Onion Rings (p. 62)

Lemon-wrapped Walleye

Serves 6

For an experienced hunting and fishing guide such as Ken Campbell of Harrington, Québec, preparing fish becomes almost second nature. Working from one of Club Caesar's outpost camps, Ken has prepared more great Canadian shore lunches and camp fish dinners than he can remember. His clients go crazy for a sumptuous yet surprisingly simple walleye dish done in extra-virgin olive oil. Then, for a taste of something special, Ken treats his guests to an irresistible dipping sauce made from chili and sugar; he calls it the "Guide's Secret Sauce." (I would offer the recipe, but it is a heavily guarded secret.) On days when larger walleye are available, Ken takes things to a whole other level with a batch of melt-in-your-mouth walleye cheeks. Apparently there is more to being a successful guide than just knowing how to locate and catch fish and game, as Ken Campbell demonstrates.

> **6 × 12 to 14 oz (340 to 400 g) walleye fillets**
> **salt and pepper, to taste**
> **2 garlic cloves, minced**
> **2 lemons, thinly sliced**

Preheat grill to medium-high. Lay out six 12-inch (30 cm) pieces of foil. Place 1 fillet on each piece of foil and sprinkle with salt, pepper and garlic. Top each fillet with 2 lemon slices. Wrap foil securely around each fillet to seal fish in. Place foil packets on grill and cook slowly for at least 15 minutes, turning packets often, until fish flakes easily with a fork. Transfer foil packets to plates and serve. Use caution when opening packets.

Baked Whitefish Florentine

Serves 4

The lake whitefish is one of the lesser-known coldwater fish species found in Canada, yet it is still one of the most important. At one time, whitefish was the most important commercial fish species in the country. They are found mostly in cold, northern lakes and are often associated with the lake trout because they share a similar habitat. The lake whitefish is a close relative of the trout and is often caught on lake bottoms by ice fishermen during the wintertime. The whitefish's flaky white meat and mild taste make it an ideal choice for a variety of dishes.

2 cups (500 mL) chopped spinach
1/2 cup (125 mL) breadcrumbs
1/3 cup (75 mL) cholesterol-free egg substitute (or 2 eggs)
1/2 cup (125 mL) chopped onion
1 tsp (5 mL) garlic powder
6 whitefish fillets (about 1 1/2 lbs [680 g] total)

1/2 cup (125 mL) white wine
2 Tbsp (30 mL) melted butter
2 Tbsp (30 mL) lemon juice
1 tsp (5 mL) paprika

1 1/2 cups (375 mL) steamed spinach, well drained

Preheat oven to 350°F (175°C) and grease shallow baking dish. Combine spinach, breadcrumbs, egg substitute, onion and garlic powder in bowl. Arrange fillets in prepared baking dish and spoon spinach mixture on centre of each fillet. Stir wine, butter and lemon juice in bowl or glass measuring cup and pour over fish. Sprinkle with paprika and bake for 25 minutes until fish flakes easily with a fork.

Place steamed spinach on serving platter and top with fish. Serve with Penne Pasta Salad, p. 166, or Rice Salad, p. 167.

Grilled Whitefish

Serves 6

At one time, whitefish was the most important commercial fish found in Canada. The Great Lakes alone produced upwards of 18 million pounds (8 million kilograms) of whitefish per year during the early 1960s. Lake whitefish were caught commercially using gillnets and trap nets and marketed in the 1 to 5 pound (0.5 to 2.3 kilogram) range. Although the commercial whitefish industry is not what it used to be, sport fishing for whitefish remains popular.

2 lbs (900 g) whitefish fillets
2 green peppers, sliced
2 onions, sliced

1/4 cup (60 mL) melted butter
2 Tbsp (30 mL) lemon juice
2 tsp (10 mL) salt
1 tsp (5 mL) paprika
pepper, to taste

Preheat grill to medium-high. Cut fish into 6 portions. Cut foil into six 12 × 12 inch pieces and grease lightly. Place 1 portion of fish, skin side down, on each piece of foil and top with green pepper and onions.

Mix remaining ingredients in bowl and pour over fish. Seal foil securely around each fillet. Place packets on grill about 5 inches (12 cm) from heat. Cook for 45 to 60 minutes until fish flakes easily with a fork.

Try with This  ## Mango Barbecue Sauce

Makes 2 1/2 cups (625 mL)

1 ripe mango, peeled, pitted and cut into small cubes
1 cup (250 mL) prepared mango chutney
1 cup (250 mL) finely chopped onion
1 Tbsp (15 mL) minced garlic
1 × 28 oz (796 mL) can peeled plum tomatoes,
    crushed, with juices
2 Tbsp (30 mL) cider vinegar
1 Tbsp (15 mL) molasses
1 tsp (5 mL) Tabasco sauce

In large saucepan, combine all ingredients. Cover and simmer over low for about 20 minutes until sauce thickens. Cool slightly. Put sauce in food processor or blender and purée until smooth. Great as dipping sauce for a variety of wild fish.

Crispy Whitefish

Serves 4

Lake whitefish are an extremely mild-tasting fish that many people avoid cooking because they are unclear how to properly season them. One challenge when cooking whitefish is getting flavouring into the meat, since the fish is not cooked long enough to really take on the flavour of whatever you cook it with. Simply cooking with herbs layered on top, either fresh or dried, doesn't really do the trick for whitefish. I have heard that you will have better success by first infusing herbs or spices in oil or melted butter, and then brushing them on the fish before cooking. This basting action seems to allow a natural absorption of the flavours.

4 Tbsp (60 mL) olive oil
1 shallot, diced
4 garlic cloves, minced

1 cup (250 mL) crushed cracker crumbs
1/2 tsp (2 mL) salt
1/2 tsp (2 mL) pepper
4 × 6 to 8 oz (170 to 225 g) whitefish fillets

Preheat oven to 350°F (175°C). Heat oil in large skillet over medium. Add shallot and garlic, and sauté until soft and slightly brown. Let cool for 5 minutes, then pour into mixing bowl. Add cracker crumbs and stir; season with salt and pepper. Dredge fillets in crumb mixture, applying a thick coating. Place in baking pan and bake for about 20 minutes until fish flakes easily and crust is golden brown.

Fried Clams

Serves 6

Clams often get confused with mussels, but they are different species of shellfish, each with a distinct taste and flavour. Clams are white to grey or even reddish brown (called mahogany clams) and mussels are a dark blue colour in an oblong shell. Mussel meat is typically yellow to brown with a heavier taste than clams, but they are both very good. Some clams may be eaten raw as well as cooked, whereas mussels are generally always cooked. Another difference is shell thickness. Mussels cook much faster than clams because of their thinner shells. Any way you look at it, they are both delicious!

2 1/2 cups (625 mL) clams, drained and chopped
2 eggs, lightly beaten
1 tsp (5 mL) grated onion
1 cup (250 mL) half-and-half cream

1 3/4 cups (425 mL) flour
1 Tbsp (15 mL) baking powder
1/4 tsp (1 mL) grated nutmeg
1 tsp (5 mL) salt

canola oil, for frying

Place clams in large bowl. Add eggs, onion and cream, and stir well. In another bowl, stir flour, baking powder, nutmeg and salt together, then add to clam mixture. Stir clam batter lightly to combine.

Preheat oil in large skillet. Drop batter by teaspoonfuls into oil. Fry until golden brown; drain on paper towels. Serve immediately.

Try with This  **Quick Tartar Sauce**
Makes 1 cup (250 mL)

1 cup (250 mL) mayonnaise
2 tsp (10 mL) sweet pickle relish
1 tsp (5 mL) prepared yellow mustard
1 tsp (5 mL) lemon juice

Stir ingredients together in bowl. Serve in cocktail dish.

Quick Clam Bake

Serves 4

Many people ask about the difference between clams and oysters. Both clams and oysters are a class of mollusks called bivalves. One big difference between oysters and clams, however, is that the oyster spends most its life, except its first few weeks, attached to one spot. The clam moves around throughout its life by means of a foot, a hatchet-shaped muscle that protrudes from its shell. The clam pushes its foot out, hooks it in the sand and pulls itself along. Oysters have a similar appendage when they're young, but it disappears when the oyster finds a place to settle. As far as taste goes, many people find clams to be milder than oysters, although they can be slightly chewier.

20 fresh clams, shucked and rinsed

3 Tbsp (45 mL) butter
1 garlic clove, minced
1/2 cup (125 mL) breadcrumbs
2 tsp (10 mL) chopped parsley
salt and pepper, to taste
2 Tbsp (30 mL) grated Parmesan cheese

Preheat oven to 400°F (205°C). Butter small casserole dish, or for individual servings use ramekins. Place clams in casserole dish, or divide among ramekins. Set aside.

In skillet, melt butter over medium and add garlic and breadcrumbs. Cook until mixture is golden and slightly crumbly. Remove from heat and stir in parsley, salt and pepper. Spoon mixture over clams and sprinkle with Parmesan cheese.

Bake clams for about 15 minutes until bubbly and lightly browned. Serve warm.

Crab Bisque

(see photo p. 141)

Serves 6

A couple of handy accessories should be nearby when one sets out to seriously enjoy a healthy serving of crab. A crab bib, as silly as it looks, will keep juice and bits of your favourite seafood from finding their way onto your new dress shirt. Disposable crab or lobster bibs are preferred since they can be discarded at the end of the meal. A good mallet, a shell cracker and a paring knife are also suggested. Be careful, because you would not believe the number of shellfish-related injuries that make it to the emergency room each year. Since a heavy mallet tends to splinter the shell, go easy when cracking a crab leg with such a tool. A paring knife comes in handy when trying to scrape that delicious meat from inside. These few simple tools of the trade will undoubtedly make any crab meal easier and safer.

4 ears corn
1/4 cup (60 mL) butter
3/4 cup (175 mL) chopped chives or shallots
3 garlic cloves, minced
3 1/2 cups (875 mL) chicken broth
1/2 tsp (2 mL) cayenne pepper
salt and pepper, to taste

3 Tbsp (45 mL) flour
2/3 cup (150 mL) cream (18%)
3 × 6 oz (170 g) cans crabmeat

Cut kernels from corn; set kernels aside. In large, steep-sided skillet over medium, cook butter, chives and garlic until chives soften. Slowly add corn, chicken broth, cayenne pepper, salt and pepper. Lower heat, cover and let simmer.

Stir flour and cream together in small bowl. Slowly pour into soup. Add crabmeat and let simmer for 10 minutes until slightly thick. Pour into large soup tureen and serve.

Marinated Crab Legs

(see photo p. 142)

Serves 4

In eastern Canada, the number of people directly involved in fish and shellfish processing has declined in recent years owing to the collapse of regional ground fish stocks and advances in technology. Despite this overall decline, however, there were still an estimated 32,000 workers employed in fish and shellfish processing plants in eastern Canada in 2004. Of these, an estimated 22,000 are shellfish processing workers. The crab species harvested in eastern Canada include the popular snow crab, rock crab, Jonah crab, toad crab, porcupine crab and red crab.

1 1/2 cups (375 mL) olive oil
2 garlic cloves, minced
2 tsp (10 mL) fresh oregano
2 tsp (10 mL) basil
2 tsp (10 mL) chopped parsley
1 tsp (5 mL) pepper
1/2 tsp (2 mL) salt
1/4 tsp (1 mL) dried dill

12 cooked crab legs, broken into sections at the joint
1 lemon, cut into wedges

To make marinade, combine all ingredients, except crab and lemon, in large bowl and stir until smooth. Place crab legs into large sealable container or bag. Pour marinade over crab and seal; refrigerate for at least 3 hours.

To serve, remove crab legs from marinade and allow to drain. Place on serving platter and garnish with lemon wedges.

Crab Casserole

Serves 4

In British Columbia, the Dungeness crab is the most important species of crab harvested and exploited by commercial, native and sport fishermen. Dungeness crabs occupy the eastern Pacific Ocean and range from the Aleutian Islands to Mexico, from the intertidal zone to depths of 590 feet (180 metres). The inception of the commercial fishery occurred in the 19th century, with first recorded landings in 1885. The Dungeness crab sport fishery also has a long history, with evidence to show that First Nations harvested them before the discovery of North America by Europeans. The province of British Columbia is aptly referred to as the Dungeness crab capital of Canada.

1 lb (454 g) crabmeat
1 onion, chopped
1 cup (250 mL) mayonnaise
1/2 cup (125 mL) half-and-half cream
1/2 tsp (2 mL) salt
1/2 tsp (2 mL) pepper
2 cups (500 mL) white bread cubes
   (1-inch [2.5 cm] cubes), *divided*

Preheat oven to 375°F (190°C). Combine all ingredients with 1 cup (250 mL) bread cubes in large bowl and stir until smooth. Transfer mixture to large casserole dish. Sprinkle 1 cup (250 mL) bread cubes on top and bake for 30 to 40 minutes until crispy and slightly brown on top.

Lobster with Crab Stuffing

Serves 4

Did you know that Listuguj Mi'gmaq, an aboriginal community in Gaspé, Québec, has lobster fishing rights protected under the Constitution Act of 1982? The agreement between the Mi'gmaq community and the Government of Canada states that they may fish throughout the year in Chaleur Bay and are allowed to use a maximum of 500 traps. The community of Listuguj Rangers are responsible for maintaining statistics and work in collaboration with the Department of Fisheries and Oceans fishery officers.

4 × 1 lb (454 g) live lobsters
2 Tbsp (30 mL) melted butter

1 cup (250 mL) diced celery
3/4 cup (175 mL) diced onion
1 cup (250 mL) diced crabmeat
1 cup (250 mL) mayonnaise

Preheat oven to 300°F (150°C). Cook lobster for 10 minutes in large pot of boiling, salted water. Split lobsters in half from underside, then brush melted butter over meat. Place lobsters in baking pan and bake for 10 minutes.

Meanwhile, heat saucepan over medium. Add celery, onion and crabmeat, and sauté until celery and onion are soft. Add mayonnaise to pan and mix to combine. Set aside.

Fill each lobster shell with crab mixture. Bake for 10 minutes. Serve hot with steamed white rice, or Rice Salad, p. 167.

Lobster Rolls

Serves 4

The Maritime lobster industry in this country is very concerned about conservation and is always under strict control measures. For example, lobster under the legal size limit of 3.3 inches (82.5 millimetres) carapace length must be released, along with females bearing eggs. In addition to quota controls, the lobster fishery is subject to a series of other management measures. Every lobster net must have what is called an "escape vent" to allow incidental catches and juvenile lobster to get away. Also, most of the new lobster nets are composed of biodegradable mesh, which breaks down quickly if abandoned or lost at sea. Since any wayward nets begin to rot within days, they have no ill effects on marine life.

> 1 × 1 to 1 1/2 lb (454 to 680 g) cooked lobster (*see* Tip, p. 136)
> 1 celery rib, chopped
> 1/2 red pepper, seeded and finely chopped
> 3 Tbsp (45 mL) mayonnaise
> 1/2 tsp (2 mL) Dijon mustard
> salt, to taste
>
> 4 fresh large dinner rolls
> 1 Tbsp (15 mL) butter

Remove meat from lobster and cut into small pieces. Place in large bowl with celery, red pepper, mayonnaise and mustard. Add salt and mix.

Heat skillet over medium. Cut dinner rolls in half and butter both sides. Place buttered rolls on skillet and toast until golden brown. Transfer rolls to serving platter and fill with lobster mixture.

Grilled Lobster

Serves 8

These days, Canadian lobster fishermen have a personal interest in management and resource sustainability of the species. Many of the larger lobster companies operate vessels with sophisticated habitat mapping equipment that ensures only specified areas are being fished. Stringent quality control practices are carried out on every fishing boat and in processing plants as well. Everyone in the industry does their utmost to keep close tabs on our Atlantic lobster, a precious natural resource. It is a Canadian tradition worth conserving for the future.

1 cup (250 mL) butter
2 Tbsp (30 mL) chopped shallots

4 × 1 lb (454 g) lobsters (*see* Tip)

salt and pepper, to taste
1 lemon, quartered

Preheat grill to medium. Melt butter in small saucepan and add shallots; shallots; saute for 2 to 3 minutes, and set aside.

Split lobsters; remove intestines, stomach and gills from body cavities, leaving empty shells. Remove claws where they attach to bodies. Crack claws, remove meat and place it in shells.

Place lobsters on grill and cook for about 20 minutes, basting with shallot butter, until meat is done (it will be firm and opaque). Be careful not to overcook.

Place lobsters on platter and season with salt and pepper. Serve with remaining shallot butter and lemon quarters.

 COOKING LOBSTER

To cook live lobsters, plunge them into a large pot of boiling, salted water. Cook, covered, for about 15 minutes. Use tongs to remove them from the pot. Alternatively, buy cooked lobsters from your seafood grocer.

Lobster Bisque

Serves 4

The most memorable lobster meal my wife and I ever enjoyed was in the lovely little town of Montague, Prince Edward Island, back in 1996. My childhood friend Mike Davis was living there at the time and invited us over for a traditional PEI meal. The Confederation Bridge was in its final stages of completion, so we even had the opportunity to take the ferry across to the island. I don't know if it was the garlic, but that particular dinner of steamed lobster with white rice and garlic butter left a lasting impression that I remember to this day. The lobsters we ate that night were easily 3 to 4 pounds (1.4 to 1.8 kilograms) apiece, steamed to perfection in natural brine the way many easterners do, and served in the heart of the Maritimes. It is just something one never forgets.

1 Tbsp (15 mL) butter
3 Tbsp (45 mL) finely diced onion
2 Tbsp (30 mL) finely diced green peppers
2 Tbsp (30 mL) finely diced yellow peppers
4 to 6 oz (115 to 170 g) cooked lobster meat (*see* Tip, p. 136)

1/3 cup (75 mL) white wine
1/3 cup (75 mL) chicken stock
1 cup (250 mL) cream (18%)
salt and pepper, to taste

saltines or oyster crackers, to serve

Heat butter in large saucepan over medium-high. Add onion and green and yellow peppers, and cook until tender. Add lobster meat and sauté for 2 to 3 minutes.

Add wine and chicken stock. Reduce heat and add cream. Season with salt and pepper, and simmer until thickened. Serve in warmed bowls with saltines or oyster crackers.

Traditional Lobster Casserole

Serves 6

When the early Europeans explored eastern Canada, lobsters were so common that Europeans reported picking them up randomly along the shore at low water. Today, lobsters are caught in baited traps or pots. Most traps are brought ashore in the coldest part of the winter at a time when lobster fishermen are less likely to interfere with scallop draggers. Traps may be set individually, in pairs or in trawls of 10 to 25 traps. The bait used is usually salted or fresh herring, but other fish species may also be added to the mixture. The lobsters are clamped with rubber bands as soon as they are removed from the traps. At the end of the day, they're hauled ashore and placed in wooden lobster crates that hold about 100 pounds (45 kilograms) of live lobsters.

3 Tbsp (45 mL) butter
3 Tbsp (45 mL) flour
3/4 tsp (4 mL) dry mustard
1 tsp (5 mL) salt
1 tsp (5 mL) pepper
1 cup (250 mL) cream (18%)
1 cup (250 mL) milk
3 cups (750 mL) sliced mushrooms
3 cups (750 mL) diced, cooked lobster meat
1/4 cup (60 mL) shredded Swiss cheese
2 cups (500 mL) bread cubes (1-inch [2.5 cm] cubes)

2/3 cup (150 mL) breadcrumbs
2 Tbsp (30 mL) melted butter

Coat large casserole dish with non-stick cooking spray; set aside. In saucepan over medium, melt butter and stir in flour, dry mustard, salt and pepper. Blend until smooth. Lower heat then add cream and milk. Simmer for 5 minutes until slightly reduced. Add mushrooms, lobster meat, Swiss cheese and bread cubes. Stir until cheese has melted.

Preheat oven to 375°F (190°C). Pour lobster mixture into prepared casserole dish. Sprinkle with breadcrumbs and drizzle with melted butter. Bake for 20 to 30 minutes until top is browned.

Pan-seared Mussels

Serves 2

Being a shellfish harvester in western Canada often comes with adversity. Take the poisonous red tides, for example. Any shellfish harvested under red tide conditions could potentially become contaminated. The chances of contaminated fish ever hitting the market are slim, but it is the fishermen and those working closely with the mussels who need to be concerned. A red tide can bring with it *Vibrio parahaemolyticus* (Vp), which can cause diarrhea, cramps, nausea and vomiting if the tainted shellfish is not properly stored or cooked prior to consumption. Levels of Vp, which occurs naturally in Pacific coastal waters, rise in warmer water conditions and can concentrate in bivalve shellfish. Immediately after harvesting, shellfish should be frozen or refrigerated. Cooking shellfish is generally an effective way of preventing illness resulting from the *Vibrio* bacteria.

2 lbs (900 g) mussels, scrubbed and de-bearded (*see* p. 140)

2 Tbsp (30 mL) olive oil
1 Tbsp (15 mL) crushed garlic
2 Tbsp (30 mL) chopped chives
salt and pepper, to taste

Heat dry cast-iron pan or skillet over high for 10 minutes. Drop mussels into pan.

Mix oil, garlic and chives in bowl. When mussels have opened, pour garlic mixture over them, and season with salt and pepper. Discard any mussels that do not open. Serve immediately.

East Coast Mussels

Serves 4 to 6

Mussels are often mistaken for oysters when in reality they differ quite a bit in biology and in taste. Oysters tend to more mobile and free-moving than mussels, which are content to simply latch onto a secondary host and spend much of their life in that one spot. Both oysters and mussels are filter feeders; however, mussels are better equipped to siphon water. The biggest life-cycle difference between the two is the fact that oysters are strictly ocean dwellers while mussels can found in both fresh or salt water. When it comes to taste and flavour, it depends on the person. Some find mussels to be chewier and a bit "fishier" in flavour than oysters, but as with any dish, taste is always in the mouth of the beholder.

> 3 Tbsp (45 mL) olive oil
> 1 small white onion, finely chopped
> 4 garlic cloves, finely chopped
> 1 cup (250 mL) white wine
> 1 × 28 oz (796 mL) can plum tomatoes, chopped
> 1 Tbsp (15 mL) freshly chopped oregano
> 1 Tbsp (15 mL) freshly chopped parsley
> 4 lbs (1.8 kg) fresh mussels, scrubbed and de-bearded (*see* Tip)
> salt and pepper, to taste

Heat oil in large skillet over medium. Add onion and garlic and cook until soft. Pour in wine and reduce; then add tomatoes, oregano and parsley. Add mussels to pan. Season with salt and pepper. Cook for about 10 minutes until all mussels open. Discard any mussels that do not open. Transfer mussels to platter and coat with sauce. Serve hot.

 tip **DE-BEARDING MUSSELS**

Before you cook any mussels, remember to de-beard them. Mussels found in Canada have what is commonly called a "beard"—a group of what are actually byssal threads. These fibres can be seen protruding through the mussel's shell and need to be removed before eating. The best way to remove the beard is to use a dry towel to grasp the threads and give them a good tug towards the hinge-end of the mussel. The direction is very important: an improperly extracted beard may spell the end of your mussel. If you pull the beard out toward the opening end of the mussel, you may actually tear the mussel on the inside of the shell, which kills it instantly. Once byssal threads are properly removed, discard them right away.

Crab Bisque (p. 131)

Marinated Crab Legs (p. 132)

Mussels in Cream Sauce

Serves 6

At Halifax's Five Fishermen Restaurant and Grill, the chefs really know their mussels, and for good reason: their world-famous restaurant serves nearly 50,000 pounds (22,500 kilograms) of these delectable bivalves annually. Don Walker, the Five Fishermen corporate chef, says the key to really outstanding mussels is to keep it simple: "We buy only fresh local farmed mussels and serve them steamed with an assortment of side sauces." When purchasing mussels, Chef Walker recommends looking for full, heavy shells that are already closed, or that close easily when tapped. Good-quality mussels should "smell like the ocean" and not like fish. Although mussels will keep for several days in the refrigerator, Chef Walker says you should cook them right away to enjoy them at the height of their freshness.

2 Tbsp (30 mL) butter
1/4 cup (60 mL) sliced shallots
1/2 cup (125 mL) diced tomatoes
1 garlic clove, sliced
4 lbs (1.8 kg) mussels, scrubbed and de-bearded (*see* p. 140)
3/4 cup (175 mL) white wine
1/3 cup (75 mL) orange juice

1 cup (250 mL) cream (18%)
1/2 tsp (2 mL) salt
1/2 tsp (2 mL) pepper

Melt butter in large saucepan over medium. Add shallots, tomatoes and garlic and cook slightly. Add mussels, wine and orange juice. Cook over medium, covered, until mussels open. Transfer mussels to serving bowls as they open and keep warm in oven. Discard any mussels that do not open.

Continue simmering liquid for 10 minutes. Stir in cream, salt and pepper, and simmer until smooth and creamy. Slowly pour cream sauce over mussels in bowls and serve.

Barbecued Oysters

Serves 4

Oysters are an excellent source of protein, but unfortunately, to recall Mark Twain, the rumour that they are a powerful aphrodisiac is greatly exaggerated! It's a long-standing belief that eating raw oysters increases your libido. Oysters may have gained their reputation at a time when their contribution of vitamins and minerals to nutritionally deficient diets of the day could improve overall health, and so led to an increased sex drive. It is believed that since oysters contain dopamine—a neurotransmitter—they may have an influence on sexual desire among men and women. The passions produced from eating oysters, some experts feel, may have more to do with high levels of zinc and sugars. Rumour or not, it still provides great conversation at parties!

20 fresh oysters, in their shells

salt and pepper, to taste
juice from 1 lemon
2 cups (500 mL) seafood cocktail sauce (*see* below)

Preheat barbecue to medium-high. Arrange oysters on grill in one layer (extras can be added to grill as you remove cooked oysters). Cook oysters with lid closed for 10 to 12 minutes until they begin to open. Discard any unopened oysters after 15 minutes.

Once cooled slightly, open oysters, and remove and discard top shell. Spread out oysters on large serving platter. Season with salt and pepper. Add a couple of drops of lemon juice and a dab of seafood cocktail sauce to each oyster, and serve.

Try with This

Tangy Cocktail Sauce
Makes 2 cups (500 mL)

1/2 onion, minced
2/3 cup (150 mL) horseradish
1 1/2 cups (375 mL) ketchup
1 tsp (5 mL) lemon juice
1 Tbsp (15 mL) cider vinegar
1/2 tsp (2 mL) salt

Mix ingredients in bowl until smooth. Great with cocktail shrimp and fried shrimp.

Oyster Stew

Serves 4

Shucking oysters and eating them fresh out of the shell can only be described as an acquired taste. The people back home in Arundel, Québec, where I grew up, organized an oyster festival during the peak oyster season. Everyone in town gathered at the Maplewood Inn to celebrate the magnificent oyster in style. I will never forget my first attempt at shucking an oyster, without knowing where the hinge is located. I dug, scraped and gouged my way around that silly little thing for probably 15 minutes before Kerry Bindon showed up to demonstrate the proper technique. After a quick seminar from Mr. Bindon, I soon became quite adept at shucking oysters, just as quickly acquiring a taste for the juicy little gems in the process.

> 1/4 cup (60 mL) butter
> 1/3 cup (75 mL) chopped onion
> 1/4 cup (60 mL) chopped green pepper
> 3 Tbsp (45 mL) flour
> 1/4 tsp (1 mL) pepper
> 1 lb (454 g) shucked oysters
> 3 cups (750 mL) milk
>
> **fresh bread or dinner buns, to serve**

In medium saucepan over medium-high, melt butter and sauté onion and green pepper. Stir with spatula until soft. Add flour and pepper and continue stirring. Reduce heat and drop in oysters. Gently simmer until oysters begin to shrink slightly. Add milk and stir until smooth.

Simmer, covered, for 10 minutes until smooth consistency is reached. Serve hot with fresh bread or dinner buns.

Oysters Rockefeller

(see photo p. 159)

Serves 4

Clams, quahogs and oysters are some of the favourite items to serve for Chef Charlotte Langley of Ottawa's popular Whalesbone Oyster House. Chef Char, as she is known around the restaurant, sent me a great trick for salting and jarring soft-shell clams. She uses her own 30 percent saltwater solution and allows the clams to soak in it for a minimum of two days. She then rinses them off and completes the usual jarring procedure, which includes five minutes sanitizing the jars and lids. She adds the cold clams to the warm jars and covers them in cold water with a splash of lemon. The jars are closed again and returned to simmering water for 10 more minutes. Chef Langley suggests eating the clams the traditional way cold and straight out of the jar.

> **2 dozen fresh oysters, shucked and left in half shell**
>
> **1 Tbsp (15 mL) canola oil**
> **6 × 9 oz (255 g) bags fresh spinach, washed and chopped**
> **2 medium onions, finely chopped**
> **3 garlic cloves, finely minced**
> **2 cups (500 mL) Béchamel sauce (*see* Tip)**
> **2 cups (500 mL) breadcrumbs, for thickening**

Preheat oven to 350°F (175°C). Arrange oysters in half shells on rimmed baking sheet. Set aside.

Heat oil in skillet and sauté spinach, onion and garlic; add Béchamel sauce and mix well. Slowly sprinkle in breadcrumbs, mixing and continuing to add just enough breadcrumbs until mixture thickens. Spoon mixture on top of oysters. Bake for 15 to 18 minutes. Remove from oven and transfer to serving platter.

 tip **MAKING BÉCHAMEL SAUCE**

Béchamel (or white sauce) is one of the Mother sauces and is the basis of many recipes. A basic Béchamel sauce is quite easy. Heat 2 Tbsp (30 mL) butter in medium saucepan over low. Whisk in 2 Tbsp (30 mL) flour until smooth. Add 1 to 1 1/2 cups (250 to 375 mL) whole milk and continue whisking to remove lumps. Season with salt and pepper to taste.

Hobo Oyster Casserole

Serves 4

The oyster industry in Canada is divided between the Pacific Northwest and Atlantic Canada, where oysters are farmed commercially using several different methods. The bulk of this country's commercial oyster farming takes place in eastern Canada. Most oyster cultivation involves either the raising of oyster larvae in a hatchery or the harvesting of wild larvae that is later raised in the ocean. Oyster farmers take the larvae and arrange them on special incubation rafts positioned on the ocean floor. Since oysters are filter feeders and are very sensitive to toxins, their water quality needs to be monitored constantly. Don't let the name fool you: this dish might be called Hobo Oyster Casserole for its ease of preparation, but your guests will mistake you for a Michelin-starred chef!

> 2 dozen oysters, shucked and cut into small chunks
> 2 cups (500 mL) cracker crumbs, *divided*
> 1 × 10 oz (284 mL) can condensed cream of chicken soup
> 1/2 cup (125 mL) milk
> 1 tsp (5 mL) salt
> 1/2 tsp (2 mL) pepper

Preheat oven to 350°F (175°C) and move rack to middle of oven. Grease large casserole dish. Place oyster chunks, 1 cup (250 mL) cracker crumbs, soup and milk in casserole dish and stir until smooth. Season with salt and pepper. Sprinkle 1 cup (250 mL) cracker crumbs on top. Bake, covered, for 30 minutes. Remove cover and bake for 15 minutes more until cracker crumbs are slightly brown. Let stand 5 minutes. Serve with fresh bread and butter.

Baked Scallops

Serves 4

If you've been to Digby, Nova Scotia, you'll know that it's situated overlooking the beautiful Annapolis Basin. You may also know that Digby's main industries are fishing and tourism. The Annapolis Basin is spectacular, and it boasts some truly incredible tides that can rise as high as 35 feet (10.5 metres). The people of the town of Digby also take the Canadian scallop very seriously and make a point of honouring it every chance they get. On August 4 to 8, 2010, the town celebrated its 35th Annual Digby Scallop Days with a parade, video dance, woodsmen competition, street car show, kid's pie eating contest, queen's coronation and, of course, lots and lots of scallop eating.

> 16 scallops, rinsed and patted dry
> 5 Tbsp (75 mL) butter, melted
> 5 garlic cloves, minced
> 2 chives, chopped
> salt and pepper, to taste
> 1 cup (250 mL) breadcrumbs
> 1/4 cup (60 mL) olive oil

Preheat oven to 400°F (205°C). Place scallops, butter, garlic and chives in bowl. Season with salt and pepper and stir. Transfer to casserole dish. Combine breadcrumbs and olive oil in mixing bowl, then spread on scallops. Bake for 15 to 20 minutes until top is golden brown. Let stand for 5 minutes before serving.

Broiled Scallops

Serves 4

Eating a mild, flavourful scallop, no matter what the size, is like having a party in your mouth and everyone's invited. Scallops have been compared to lobster and crab but have a lighter and creamier taste. Scallops can be cooked in a multitude of ways. Always keep in mind that scallops take very little time to cook and will lose their delicate flavour and texture if overcooked. Scallops are done broiling when they turn opaque in colour but the centre is still slightly translucent. As with most other seafood, scallops tend to be chewy when overcooked. What one would ideally like to hear when done cooking a scallop is Chef Gordon Ramsey of *Hell's Kitchen* saying, "That scallop is cooked perfectly!"

Broiled Scallops, continued

> 2 lbs (900 g) scallops
> 1 Tbsp (15 mL) garlic salt
> 2 Tbsp (30 mL) melted butter
> 2 Tbsp (30 mL) lemon juice

Preheat broiler. Rinse scallops with cold water, pat dry with paper towel and place on baking pan. Sprinkle with garlic salt, butter and lemon juice. Broil for 5 to 8 minutes until scallops turn golden brown. Remove from oven, let stand for 5 minutes and serve.

Quick Seared Scallops

Serves 4

According to the Marine Stewardship Council, a typical Canadian scallop boat will use two dredges for catching scallops, varying in width from 15 to 17 feet (4.6 to 5.2 metres). These dredges are towed at speeds ranging from 3 to 5.5 knots for a duration ranging from 20 to 30 minutes. The scallop industry is smaller and more specialized than some other commercial fish industries in Canada, yet still contributes more than $100 million to the country's economy each year.

> 2 Tbsp (30 mL) butter
> 2 Tbsp (30 mL) canola oil
> 1 lb (454 g) fresh scallops, rinsed and patted dry
> salt and pepper, to taste
> 1 lemon, cut into wedges

Heat butter and oil in large skillet over medium-high. Season scallops with salt and pepper and place in hot skillet in single layer. Cook until opaque, turning several times. Transfer to platter and garnish with lemon wedges. Serve immediately.

Down East Broiled Scallops

Serves 12

It is a little-known fact that recreational scallop diving permits may be purchased from the Department of Fisheries and Oceans. Because only the muscle is eaten, the scallop industry is not affected by dangerous algae blooms or other toxins that can affect clams, mussels and oysters. The "meat" of a scallop is actually two muscles used to regulate opening and closing of the shells. Scallop fishing is regulated a number of ways: through licensing, designated fishing areas, seasonal closures, restricted working hours and days, minimum size of shell and minimum number of "meats" per a specific weight, dockside monitoring, recording activities in fishing logs and, in some areas, satellite tracking of vessels. Nothing goes unnoticed in the scallop fishing grounds!

> 1/4 cup (60 mL) olive oil
> 3 Tbsp (45 mL) butter
> 1 white onion, chopped
> 2 lbs (900 g) scallops, rinsed and patted dry
>
> 3 Tbsp (45 mL) flour
> salt and pepper, to taste
> 1/2 cup (125 mL) cornmeal

Grease baking dish and set aside. In large skillet over medium-high, add oil, butter and onion. Sauté for 5 minutes. Add scallops and sauté for 5 more minutes. Reduce heat, cover and simmer for 5 minutes. Remove skillet from heat. Use tongs to remove scallops and place them in prepared baking dish. Set aside.

Preheat oven to 375°F (190°C). Place skillet back on medium-high. Slowly add flour to skillet; stir until consistency is thicker. Add salt and pepper. Pour sauce in baking dish over scallops and stir slightly. Sprinkle cornmeal on top. Bake for about 45 minutes until golden brown on top. Let stand 5 minutes, then serve.

Grilled Scallops

Serves 6

Although they are rather simple to cook, there are certain rules to remember when grilling the coveted scallop. First, you must always ensure freshness—there's nothing worse than eating fish or seafood that isn't fresh. Fresh, high-quality scallops should have very little "fishy" smell to them. Experts often denote a certain sweetness in the smell of really fresh, high-quality scallops. Remember: never try cooking scallops on a grill that isn't preheated to medium-high, because they cook very quickly. Although scallops are quite easy to grill, always keep a close eye on temperature: scallops can cook in less than 4 minutes per side depending on heat. Good luck and enjoy!

3/4 cup (175 mL) butter
2/3 cup (150 mL) chopped onions
3 garlic cloves, chopped
1/4 cup (60 mL) lemon juice
1/2 tsp (2 mL) salt

2 lbs (900 g) scallops, rinsed and patted dry

Preheat non-stick grill to medium and lightly oil grate. Melt butter in saucepan over medium. Add onion and garlic and cook until soft, then remove from heat and stir in lemon juice and salt. Put scallops in bowl and pour butter mixture over top; toss to coat. Let stand for about 5 minutes.

Place scallops in fine-mesh barbecue grill or grill basket. Cook for about 5 minutes until opaque; remove from heat. Meanwhile, heat butter mixture on medium, bring to a boil and then lower heat until scallops are cooked. Pour butter over grilled scallops and serve.

Try with This  **Lemon Mayonnaise**
Makes 1 cup (250 mL)

1 cup (250 mL) mayonnaise
2 Tbsp (30 mL) chopped fresh dill
1 1/2 tsp (7 mL) chopped fresh parsley
2 tsp (10 mL) lemon juice

In small bowl, combine all ingredients. Refrigerate for at least 2 hours. Serve as dip with fish or seafood.

Shrimp Fettuccini

Serves 4

In October 2010, Gail Shea, Minister of Fisheries and Oceans, congratulated marine scientists from around the world on the completion of a global project known as the Census of Marine Life. Researchers from more than 80 countries worked to develop the first comprehensive worldwide catalogue of marine life. The 10-year initiative culminated with the international release of the results from the census in London, England. "The Census of Marine Life will greatly advance our understanding of marine species and their habitats, both in Canada and around the world," said Minister Shea. Initiatives like this one help maintain sustainability in Canada.

1 lb (454 g) fettuccine noodles

1 cup (250 mL) cream (18%)
2 Tbsp (30 mL) lemon juice, *divided*
1 lb (454 g) uncooked shrimp, peeled and de-veined (*see* Tip)
1 Tbsp (15 mL) minced chives

2 Tbsp (30 mL) olive oil
salt and pepper, to taste

Cook fettuccine according to package instructions; drain and keep warm.

Heat saucepan over low. Add cream and 1 Tbsp (15 mL) lemon juice and heat slightly; set aside. In small bowl, combine 1 Tbsp (15 mL) lemon juice, shrimp and chives; set aside.

Heat oil in large skillet over medium. Add shrimp mixture and cook until shrimp is opaque, then add warm cream mixture. Season with salt and pepper. Stir in fettuccini and lower heat. Simmer for 5 minutes and serve.

 tip PEELING AND DE-VEINING SHRIMP

Use your thumbs to peel back the sides of the shrimp shell. Slowly pull away any fibres of legs that remain once the shell has been removed. Hold the body of the shrimp and gently tug on the tail. The shell will come off with the tail. To de-vein shrimp, use a small, sharp knife to make a shallow cut down the back, exposing the vein. Pull the vein out gently with your fingers.

Grilled Marinated Shrimp

Serves 4

The only thing better than grilled shrimp is grilled shrimp served over hot coals. One mistake many outdoor chefs make is rushing the cooking fire. I can recall failing miserably at open-fire meals as a teenager until I learned the value of patience when preparing a meal outdoors. It takes between 1 and 2 hours to produce a bed of hot coals suitable for cooking. If you rush things in the hope that a mediocre-sized bed of coals will suffice, you are sadly mistaken. Prepare your fire well with paper, softwood kindling and a good, dry hardwood base. Allow the fire to burn for long enough that a thick bed of red-hot coals is produced. As I have discovered, taking your time is the key to success.

> 20 jumbo uncooked shrimp,
>   peeled and de-veined (*see* Tip, p. 152)
> 1 Tbsp (15 mL) chopped fresh rosemary
> 1 tsp (5 mL) dried whole oregano
> 1/4 cup (60 mL) chopped parsley
> 1/4 cup (60 mL) lemon juice
> 3 Tbsp (45 mL) olive oil
> 1/2 tsp (2 mL) salt
> 1/2 tsp (2 mL) pepper
>
> 1 lemon, cut into slices

Place shrimp in bowl, then add rosemary, oregano, parsley, lemon juice, olive oil, salt and pepper, and mix well. Cover and refrigerate for 2 to 3 hours.

Coat grill with oil or spray with non-stick cooking spray. Preheat grill to medium-high. Remove bowl from fridge and place shrimp, one by one, on hot grill. Cook shrimp for 4 to 5 minutes, turning regularly, until dark and slightly opaque. Remove shrimp and place on serving platter. Garnish with lemon slices.

Spicy Shrimp on the Barbie

(*see* photo p. 160)

Serves 4

In 2000, Prince Edward Island's Northern Shrimp Management Plan announced a new, expanded harvest allocation of 1500 metric tonnes of northern shrimp. As part of the new Management Plan, a non-profit third-party organization called the PEI Atlantic Shrimp Corp. Inc. (PEIASC) was established to keep close tabs on the province's shrimp quota. The quota was granted with the provision that the benefits from the quota would go towards the PEI fishery as a whole. The company's membership included a representative from the province of Prince Edward Island, the PEI Seafood Processors Association, the PEI Council of Professional Fish Harvesters, the University of Prince Edward Island and an independent chairperson. It was a new sign of the times for the PEI shrimp industry.

20 large uncooked shrimp, peeled and de-veined (*see* Tip, p. 152)
1/2 cup (125 mL) plain yogurt
1 Tbsp (15 mL) finely chopped mint leaves
1 tsp (5 mL) salt

1 Tbsp (15 mL) chopped fresh ginger
2 garlic cloves, crushed
1 tsp (5 mL) chili powder
1 tsp (5 mL) turmeric
1 tsp (5 mL) ground coriander

2 lemons, sliced, for garnish

Place shrimp in large bowl or sealable plastic bag. Combine yogurt, mint and salt in small bowl and pour over shrimp; let stand for 5 minutes. In same bowl, mix together remaining ingredients except lemon slices. Add to shrimp and refrigerate for 1 hour.

Heat barbecue to medium-high. Remove shrimp from marinade and place in grilling basket on top of grill rack, flipping basket so shrimp cook on both sides. They are done when they change from translucent to opaque. Transfer shrimp to serving platter and garnish with lemon slices. Serve immediately.

Shrimp Stir-fry with Veggies

Serves 4

Did you know that our most common shrimp, the *Pandalus borealis* or northern shrimp, are actually hermaphrodites, starting out their lives as male and becoming female later on? After the first or second year of growth, the male shrimp's testicles turn to ovaries and they finish their lives as females. Once the female ovaries are fully developed by the fourth or fifth year, mating takes place. In colder waters, the shrimp's growth and maturity are delayed and their life spans are lengthened. Northern shrimp, like Atlantic lobster, go through moulting periods where they shed their shells, absorb water and then develop a new soft shell. Northern shrimp—often mistakenly called prawns— are fished extensively in eastern Canada, where they achieved Sustainable Fishing Certification (SFC) in 2008. The northern shrimp fishery is the first in Canada to achieve the coveted sustainability certification.

3 Tbsp (45 mL) water
1 Tbsp (15 mL) cornstarch
1 Tbsp (15 mL) soy sauce
1 tsp (5 mL) sugar

2 Tbsp (30 mL) vegetable oil
1 small head Chinese cabbage, coarsely chopped
1 bunch green onions,
   sliced diagonally into 1/4-inch (6 mm) pieces

1 lb (454 g) medium uncooked shrimp,
   peeled and de-veined (*see* Tip, p. 152)
1/4 tsp (1 mL) ground ginger
1 × 15 oz (425 mL) can straw mushrooms

In small bowl, combine water, cornstarch, soy sauce and sugar. Set aside.

In wok, preheat oil until hot. Add cabbage and green onions and stir-fry for 2 minutes. Add 1 Tbsp (15 mL) cornstarch mixture, and cook for 1 minute. Remove cabbage mixture and set aside. Place shrimp and ginger in wok and stir-fry for 5 minutes. Add mushrooms and remaining cornstarch mixture and continue to fry for 2 minutes.

Place warm cabbage on individual plates, top with shrimp mixture and serve.

Cauliflower with Cheese Sauce

Serves 4

1 × 3 lb (1.4 kg) head cauliflower, cut into florets

1/4 cup (60 mL) skim milk powder
1/4 cup (60 mL) flour
1/4 tsp (1 mL) salt
1/2 tsp (2 mL) garlic powder
1/2 tsp (2 mL) oregano
1/4 tsp (1 mL) basil
1/8 tsp (0.5 mL) pepper

1 1/2 cups (375 mL) skim milk
1/2 cup (125 mL) grated Cheddar cheese

Steam cauliflower until tender. Transfer to serving platter, cover loosely with foil and set aside.

In medium saucepan over medium, whisk together milk powder, flour, salt, garlic powder, oregano, basil and pepper until smooth. Whisk in milk; add grated cheese and heat until melted. Pour cheese sauce over cauliflower florets and serve.

Mixed Vegetable Sauté

Serves 6

1 medium yellow summer squash, diced
1/2 cup (125 mL) chopped carrot
1/2 cup (125 mL) diced zucchini
3 shallots, chopped
1 Tbsp (15 mL) olive oil
salt and pepper, to taste
1 Tbsp (15 mL) fresh tarragon

In frying pan over medium, combine squash, carrot, zucchini, shallots and oil. Sprinkle with salt and pepper. Cook, stirring often, until vegetables are tender. Before serving, toss with tarragon.

Green Beans, Celery and Almonds

Serves 4

1 lb (454 g) green beans

1/2 small onion, sliced
3 to 4 celery ribs, cut diagonally into slices
2 tsp (10 mL) butter, *divided*
salt and pepper, to taste

1/4 cup (60 mL) slivered almonds

Parboil beans for 3 minutes. Rinse under cold water, and cut into 3-inch (7.5 cm) lengths.

In large frying pan, sauté onion and celery in 1 tsp (5 mL) butter until crispy and tender. Add beans and stir to combine; sprinkle with salt and pepper.

In small frying pan, melt 1 tsp (5 mL) butter and sauté almonds until golden brown, stirring constantly. Add to beans and serve.

Wild Fiddleheads in the Pan

Serves 4 to 8

1/4 cup (60 mL) butter
1/2 cup (125 mL) finely minced onion
1 Tbsp (15 mL) minced garlic
1 lb (454 g) fiddleheads, rinsed
salt and pepper, to taste
1 Tbsp (15 mL) lemon juice
1 Tbsp (15 mL) white sugar
1 tsp (5 mL) paprika

Heat butter in frying pan and fry onion and garlic for about 2 minutes. Stir in fiddleheads. Sprinkle with salt, pepper, lemon juice, sugar and paprika and sauté for about 3 to 5 minutes until fiddleheads are tender.

Potato Skins

Serves 4

4 large baking potatoes, scrubbed

oil, for deep-frying

salt and pepper, to taste
sour cream mixed with chives (optional)
shredded cheese (optional)

Preheat oven to 375°F (190°C). Stab potatoes each several times with a fork and bake for about 1 hour until tender.

Heat oil in deep-fryer to 400°F (205°C). Cut cooked potatoes lengthwise. Scoop potato flesh out and set aside for some other use. Cut skins in half again. Fry potato skins in hot oil for about 2 to 3 minutes until brown and crispy.

Use slotted spoon to transfer potato skins from deep-fryer to paper towels to drain. Sprinkle with salt and pepper. Serve with sour cream and chives, or your favourite toppings. If using shredded cheese, place potato skins topped with cheese under oven broiler to melt.

Garlic Mashed Potatoes

Serves 4

2 lbs (900 g) potatoes, peeled and halved

3 garlic cloves, chopped
3 wild garlic bulbs, chopped (optional)
1 Tbsp (15 mL) butter

1/2 cup (125 mL) half-and-half cream
1/2 tsp (2 mL) salt
1/4 tsp (1 mL) pepper

Boil potatoes in salted water until cooked; drain and return to pot. In small skillet, fry garlic and wild garlic in butter until cooked.

Add cooked garlic, cream, salt and pepper to potatoes. Mash with hand mixer until potatoes are light and fluffy. Serve immediately.

158

Oysters Rockefeller (p. 146)

Spicy Shrimp on the Barbie (p. 154)

Baked Butternut Squash

Serves 6

1 × 4 lbs (1.8 kg) butternut squash, peeled, seeded and cubed
1 small onion, minced
1/4 cup (60 mL) olive oil
3/4 cup (175 mL) crumbled blue cheese
3/4 cup (175 mL) breadcrumbs, *divided*
salt and pepper, to taste

Preheat oven to 425°F (220°C). In large bowl, combine squash, onion, oil, blue cheese and 1/4 cup (60 mL) of breadcrumbs. Add salt and pepper. Place mixture in large baking dish, sprinkle with 1/2 cup (125 mL) breadcrumbs and bake for 35 to 40 minutes until lightly browned.

Oven Risotto

Serves 6

2 Tbsp (30 mL) butter
2 shallots, diced
2 cups (500 mL) Arborio rice
1/2 cup (125 mL) white wine
6 cups (1.5 L) chicken stock
1/2 cup (125 mL) grated Parmesan cheese
salt and pepper, to taste

Preheat oven to 400°F (205°C). In large saucepan over medium, sauté butter and shallots until soft. Stir in rice and wine. Simmer, uncovered, for 5 minutes. Stir in chicken stock and sprinkle in Parmesan cheese. Slowly pour mixture into large casserole dish. Bake, covered, for 20 to 25 minutes until rice is *al dente* (firm but not crunchy). Season with salt and pepper.

Jasmine Rice with Ginger and Sesame

Serves 4

1 cup (250 mL) uncooked jasmine rice

1/4 cup (60 mL) extra-virgin olive oil
1/3 cup (75 mL) fresh ground ginger
1/3 cup (75 mL) sesame seeds

Cook rice as per package directions.

In small frying pan, heat oil over medium. Add ginger and sauté lightly. Add sesame seeds and lightly toast (add another 1 Tbsp [15 mL] olive oil if required). Once rice is cooked, stir in sesame seed mixture and serve.

Autumn Apple Coleslaw

Serves 4

2 Tbsp (30 mL) butter
1/4 tsp (1 mL) fennel seeds, crushed
1 cup (250 mL) thinly sliced sweet onion
1 tsp (5 mL) salt
1/2 red cabbage, finely shredded
1/2 cup (125 mL) apple juice
1 apple, peeled and grated
1 tsp (5 mL) apple cider vinegar

In large saucepan, melt butter and add fennel seeds, onion and salt. Cook over medium for about 2 minutes. Add cabbage and cook for 1 minute. Add apple juice, reduce heat and cover. Allow to simmer for 15 minutes, stirring every couple of minutes. Stir in apple and vinegar and simmer for 2 minutes. Remove from heat, and let sit, covered, for 5 minutes. Serve.

Basmati Rice

Serves 4

2 Tbsp (30 mL) butter, *divided*
1/4 cup (60 mL) diced celery
2 garlic cloves, minced
1/2 cup (125 mL) diced onion
1/2 cup (125 mL) chopped fresh sorrel leaves
1 tsp (5 mL) grated lemon peel
1 cup (250 mL) brown basmati rice, rinsed

1 cup (250 mL) frozen peas, thawed and rinsed
salt and pepper, to taste

In rice cooker, melt 1 Tbsp (15 mL) butter. (To cook this dish without a rice cooker, *see* Tip.) Add celery, garlic and onion and sauté until tender. Add sorrel, lemon peel and rice, and stir to coat. Add enough water to top rice by 1 inch (2.5 cm; about 3 cups [750 mL] water).

Once rice is ready (rice maker will beep or a light will go off), add peas and 1 Tbsp (15 mL) butter. Season with salt and pepper.

 tip
To prepare Basmati Rice without a rice cooker, melt 1 Tbsp (15 mL) butter in medium saucepan. Add celery, garlic and onion; sauté until tender. Add sorrel, lemon zest and rice, and stir to coat. Add about 3 cups (750 mL) water; bring to boil. Reduce heat to simmer and cover. Cook for 30 to 45 minutes until rice is tender. Add peas and 1 Tbsp (15 mL) butter; season with salt and pepper.

Garlic Couscous

Serves 4

1 Tbsp (15 mL) extra-virgin olive oil
1 garlic clove, minced
1 cup (250 mL) couscous
1 1/3 cups (325 mL) chicken broth
1/3 cup (75 mL) freshly grated Parmesan cheese
salt and pepper, to taste

In medium saucepan, cook oil and garlic over medium-high until bubbles form. Add couscous and chicken broth and bring to a boil. Reduce heat to low and simmer on low for 3 minutes. Add Parmesan cheese, salt and pepper, and serve.

Sautéed Zucchini and Cherry Tomatoes

Serves 4

1 Tbsp (15 mL) olive oil
2 zucchini, cut into 1-inch (2.5 cm) pieces
1 garlic clove, minced
1/4 tsp (1 mL) dried oregano
1/4 tsp (1 mL) salt
pinch of hot pepper flakes
pinch of sugar
1 1/2 cups (375 mL) cherry tomatoes, halved
1 Tbsp (15 mL) thinly sliced green onion
2 tsp (10 mL) red-wine vinegar

Heat oil in large frying pan over medium-high. Add zucchini, garlic, oregano, salt, hot pepper flakes and sugar. Cook for about 3 minutes, stirring, until softened. Add tomatoes and cook for 5 minutes. Add green onion and vinegar, stir well and serve.

Barb's Macaroni Salad

Serves 6

1 × 9 oz (225 g) package uncooked elbow macaroni

3/4 cup (175 mL) mayonnaise
1 tsp (5 mL) sugar
1 tsp (5 mL) salt
1/4 tsp (1 mL) pepper
1/4 cup (60 mL) sliced shallots
2 red peppers, chopped

Prepare macaroni according to package instructions. Be sure to cook *al dente* (firm but not crunchy). Drain and place in large salad bowl.

In separate bowl, mix remaining ingredients. Add to macaroni and toss to blend. Cover and refrigerate for at least 1 hour before serving.

Classic Caesar Salad

Serves 6

6 Romaine lettuce hearts

1/4 cup (60 mL) olive oil
3 Tbsp (45 mL) + 1/4 cup (60 mL) grated Parmesan cheese
1 Tbsp (15 mL) white-wine vinegar
2 tsp (10 mL) Dijon mustard
3 garlic cloves, minced
1/2 tsp (2 mL) salt
1/2 tsp (2 mL) pepper
3 Tbsp (45 mL) mayonnaise

2 1/2 cups (625 mL) croutons

Cut lettuce lengthwise at 1-inch (2.5 cm) intervals. Place in extra-large salad bowl.

In separate bowl, whisk oil, 3 Tbsp (45 mL) Parmesan cheese, vinegar, mustard, garlic, salt, pepper and mayonnaise until smooth.

Add dressing, croutons and 1/4 cup (60 mL) Parmesan cheese to lettuce; toss to combine.

Creamy Potato Salad

Serves 6

1 × 9 oz (250 g) block of cream cheese
1/3 cup (75 mL) milk
1 green pepper, chopped
2 1/2 lbs (1.1 kg) potatoes, quartered, boiled and drained

In medium saucepan over medium, heat cream cheese, milk and green pepper, stirring until blended. Let stand for 5 minutes. Place potatoes in large bowl; slowly pour cream cheese mixture over top and gently mix until smooth. Cover and refrigerate for 2 hours before serving.

Penne Pasta Salad

Serves 4 to 6

1 lb (454 g) penne pasta, cooked according to
    package directions
2 red onions, chopped
1 red pepper, finely minced

3/4 cup (175 mL) olive oil
1 Tbsp (15 mL) balsamic vinegar
1/4 cup (60 mL) fresh parsley, coarsely chopped
3 Tbsp (45 mL) grated Parmesan cheese
1/2 tsp (2 mL) basil
1/2 tsp (2 mL) minced fresh rosemary
1/4 tsp (1 mL) thyme
3 garlic cloves, minced
salt and pepper, to taste

Drain pasta and place in large bowl with onions and red pepper; stir to combine.

Mix remaining ingredients in separate bowl, then taste and adjust seasoning. Pour over pasta and refrigerate for several hours before serving.

Sides and Salads

Rice Salad

Serves 4 to 6

2 cups (500 mL) cooked rice
1 cup (250 mL) peas
1/4 cup (60 mL) chopped green pepper
1/4 cup (60 mL) chopped celery
1 Tbsp (15 mL) finely chopped green onion

1 Tbsp (15 mL) vegetable oil
1/4 tsp (1 mL) ground nutmeg
1/2 tsp (2 mL) salt
1/2 tsp (2 mL) pepper

Combine rice, peas, green pepper, celery and onion in large bowl. Mix remaining ingredients together in separate bowl. Pour into rice bowl and mix. Refrigerate for 2 hours before serving.

Quick Slaw

Serves 4

1 small head green cabbage, thinly sliced
1/4 cup (60 mL) red cabbage, thinly sliced
1 medium carrot, shredded

2/3 cup (150 mL) mayonnaise
2 Tbsp (30 mL) + 2 tsp (10 mL) sugar
2/3 tsp (3 mL) salt
2/3 tsp (3 mL) celery seed
2 Tbsp (30 mL) + 2 tsp (10 mL) white vinegar
3/4 tsp (4 mL) mustard
dash of white pepper

Place green and red cabbage and carrot in large bowl; mix and set aside. Combine remaining ingredients in small bowl and mix well. Pour part of dressing into cabbage mixture to moisten; refrigerate until ready to serve. Serve additional dressing on the side.

Canadian Fruit Salad

Serves 6

2 Cortland apples
2 McIntosh apples
2 Bartlett pears
1 banana
1/2 lb (225 g) white grapes
1/2 cup (125 mL) toasted almond slivers

1 cup (250 mL) vanilla yogurt
1 tsp (5 mL) cinnamon
1/4 tsp (1 mL) ground ginger
1/2 tsp (2 mL) nutmeg
1 Tbsp (15 mL) apple cider

Peel and core apples and pears and cut into 1-inch (2.5 cm) pieces. Peel banana and slice about 1/2-inch (12 mm) thick. Cut grapes in half. Place fruit in large bowl; add almond slivers and set aside.

In small bowl, combine remaining ingredients. Pour over fruit mixture; stir to combine.

Potato Salad

Serves 4

1 1/2 lb (680 g) potatoes

1/4 cup (60 mL) sugar
1 tsp (5 mL) flour
1/2 tsp (2 mL) dry mustard
1/8 tsp (0.5 mL) salt

1 egg, well beaten
1/4 cup (60 mL) vinegar
1/4 cup (60 mL) water
1 tsp (5 mL) olive oil

4 shallots, white parts only, chopped
salt and pepper, to taste

Potato Salad, continued

Boil potatoes until tender, then drain and set aside to cool.

In saucepan, combine sugar, flour, dry mustard and salt. Once well mixed, add egg, vinegar, water and oil. Cook over medium heat, stirring occasionally, for about 10 minutes until thickened. (Dressing can also be prepared in the microwave; *see* Tip for directions.)

Transfer to large bowl. Add chopped shallots. Cut potatoes into bite-sized pieces and add. Combine well; season with salt and pepper. Refrigerate until ready to serve.

 tip Alternatively, combine dressing ingredients (sugar, flower, dry mustard, salt, egg, vinegar, water and oil) in microwavable bowl and microwave on high for 5 minutes.

Stovetop Capellini
Serves 4

2 cups (500 mL) uncooked capellini

3 Tbsp (45 mL) olive oil
3 garlic cloves, chopped
2 × 14 oz (398 mL) cans diced tomatoes, drained
juice from 1 lemon
1/8 tsp (0.5 mL) salt
1/8 tsp (0.5 mL) pepper
1 lemon, cut into 1/4-inch (6 mm) slices, for garnish

Cook capellini according to package directions; drain and keep warm.

Cook oil and garlic in skillet over medium for 5 minutes. Add tomatoes, lemon juice, salt and pepper. Reduce heat; simmer for 5 minutes. Add pasta to skillet, stir well, then cover and simmer for 5 minutes more. Garnish with lemon. Serve hot with any fish or seafood dish (see Walnut-fried Bass, p. 25).

Greek Couscous Salad

Serves 4

1/2 cup (125 mL) couscous
1/2 cup (125 mL) boiling water

4 tsp (20 mL) extra-virgin olive oil
2 Tbsp (30 mL) red-wine vinegar
1/4 tsp (1 mL) salt
1/4 tsp (1 mL) pepper

1 cup (250 mL) plum tomatoes, diced
1/4 cup (60 mL) black olives, sliced
1 Tbsp (15 mL) fresh oregano, chopped
1/2 cup (125 mL) feta cheese, crumbled

Place couscous in large heat-proof bowl and pour boiling water over top. Let stand for 10 minutes until water has disappeared. In small bowl, combine oil, vinegar, salt and pepper; pour over couscous. Add remaining ingredients, toss and serve.

Citrus Brussels Sprouts

Serves 4

16 Brussels sprouts, trimmed and cut in half
1 Tbsp (15 mL) butter
1/4 tsp (1 mL) ground ginger
salt and pepper, to taste
1 tsp (5 mL) grated orange rind
1/4 cup (60 mL) orange juice
1/2 tsp (2 mL) cornstarch

In vegetable steamer (or in medium pot), blanch Brussels sprouts for about 5 minutes.

In large frying pan, melt butter and add Brussels sprouts, ginger, salt and pepper. Add orange rind, orange juice and cornstarch; cook, stirring constantly, for 3 minutes until sauce has thickened. Serve immediately.

Recipe Index

171

173

175

About the Author

Growing up in a family-owned hotel in the Laurentian Mountains of rural Québec, Jeff was introduced to the outdoors and great cooking at a very young age, falling in love with both instantly. Over the years, he has made the great outdoors a focal point for his life's work. Jeff has a degree in environmental management as well as fish and wildlife biology. He is an award-winning member of the Outdoor Writers of Canada and has contributed to several Canadian and American publications over the years. He currently writes for Newfoundland's popular *Outdoor Sportsman* magazine and *Outdoor Canada* magazine, and has a regular column in *Bounder Magazine*. His first book, *Weird Facts about Fishing*, was released in 2010, and he writes a popular blog, *The Outdoors Guy*, for the *Ottawa Sun*.

Jeff has travelled to each and every province from coast to coast—hunting, fishing, camping and enjoying the fruits of his labour. He describes himself as the consummate conservationist and family-man, and describes his cooking as down to earth, simple, and about as Canadian as you can get. Jeff spent a lot of time at his uncle's famous steakhouse in the mountains of Québec, and picked up copious down-home tips along the way. He brings with him an in-depth knowledge of nature and conservation and a genuine love and passion for the outdoors—from the field to the table.